Israel

D1304262

- A  in the text denotes a highly recommended sight
- A complete A–Z of practical information starts on p.104
- Extensive mapping on cover flaps and throughout text

Berlitz Publishing Company, Inc.
Princeton Mexico City London Eschborn Singapore

Original Text:	Paul Murphy
Photography:	Paul Murphy
Editors:	Alan Tucker, Stephen Brewer
Layout:	Media Content Marketing, Inc.
Cartography:	GeoSystems Global Corporation
Cover photo:	Courtesy of the Israel Ministry of Tourism

Although we make every effort to ensure the accuracy of all information in this book, changes do occur. If you find an error in this guide, please let our editors know by writing to us at Berlitz Publishing Company, 400 Alexander Park, Princeton, NJ 08540-6306. A postcard will do.

ISBN 2-8315-6307-0

Revised 1998 – Second Printing November 2000

Printed in Italy
020/011 RP

CONTENTS

Israel and the Israelis	**7**
A Brief History	**10**
Where to Go	**21**
Jerusalem	21
The West Bank	40
Tel Aviv and Jaffa	44
The Coastal Strip	50
Haifa and the Northern Coast	53
The Galilee	59
The Dead Sea	67
The Negev	72
Excursions beyond Israel	77

What to Do   81

Shopping   81
Sports   84
Entertainment   89
Children's Israel   93

Eating Out   95

Index   101

Handy Travel Tips   104

Hotels and Restaurants   129

Maps

Jerusalem Old City   27
Tel Aviv–Jaffa   45

ISRAEL

ISRAEL AND
THE ISRAELIS

Israel is many things to many people: a land of hope, wonder, faith, salvation, contradiction, and sometimes despair. Although Israel is only now 50 years old, the roots of its three prime religious faiths (Judaism, Islam, and Christianity) stretch back over many millennia, and some of its ancient settlements are amongst the oldest on earth.

Abraham, the first Jewish Patriarch, led his people here in search of "the land of milk and honey"; Jesus Christ was born, lived, ministered, and died here; and Mohammed, the founder of Islam, visited Jerusalem during his heavenly "Night Journey." Each religion and sect—Jews, Muslims (including Druse), Christians (including Armenian and Eastern Orthodox, Catholics, Protestants, Samaritans, and Copts), Baha'i, and several more—claims some piece of this sacred earth. Each faith worships a single god and recognizes elements of the others' beliefs. Sometimes more than one denomination shares one church. The church may then be marked out to designate where worshippers of the various denominations take their place.

This giddying confluence of distinct religions is matched only by the diversity of the population. As a largely immigrant society, the State of Israel provides home to people from over 80 countries around the world. Nearly half the Jewish inhabitants hail from overseas, and they have brought with them many of the accumulated customs and cultural traditions of their former homes.

In the face of such plurality it's hard to characterize Israel. This is a land where different and sometimes conflicting traditions continue to matter despite heavy odds. Not so much a melting-pot as a "land of unlimited impossibilities," Israel compresses a host of sights and lifestyles into a small area, offering a cornucopia of experiences for visitors.

Preeminent among the attractions is Jerusalem. The Temple Mount area is the geographical heart of Judaism. The city has drawn Christian visitors, sometimes heavily armed, ever since the proclamation of the "Holy Land" and development of the first Christian sites for pilgrims in the fifth century. You'll find that the Old City's myriad colours, sounds, smells, and tastes stir the senses; the Temple Mount's architecture can take your breath away; pilgrims tracing Christ's journey to Calvary along the Via Dolorosa remain a deeply moving sight; and the views from the Mount of Olives are stunning. For Christians seeking spiritual refreshment, there are countless churches to visit, including the Church of the Holy Sepulchre, the Basilica of the Annunciation (in Nazareth), and the Church of the Nativity (in Bethlehem), just to mention the most famous. Muslims revere the sites on the Temple Mount: the Dome of the Rock and El-Aksa Mosque. Even when these sights are bustling with visitors you're likely to find them compelling.

However, Jerusalem is only a starting point—beyond the capital lie more visitor attractions per square mile than in any other country in the world, beckoning not only pilgrims, historians, and archaeologists, but also hikers, ornithologists, scuba-divers, windsurfers, and many others. Israel is so compact you can cram enough variety of activities into a week to satisfy almost every taste.

Indeed, should you decide to go slow on culture, you'll find Israel a splendid place for leisurely sun-worshipping. In recent years the country has begun to realise its considerable potential for beach-style tourism. The fast-paced metropolis of Tel Aviv boasts beautiful white sands, while other parts of the country have their own unique features. It is perfectly feasible to spend a fortnight in Eilat, exploring the Red Sea, lying on the beaches, journeying into the Negev Desert—and never see a religious building or an archaeological site.

After an exhausting day on the go or at the beach, you can rest assured that you'll be able to relax in comfortable hotels, hospices, and restaurants. Israelis are delighted that people from everywhere visit their country, and welcome you with genuine warmth. Nor are you likely to encounter a language problem, as English is taught in all schools and is widely spoken.

It has been suggested that it's impossible for any foreigner to understand the Israeli psyche. Possibly no other country has had such a turbulent history. Visits to Masada and Yad Vashem (the Holocaust Museum) may give you an inkling of the capacity for tragedy and heroism embodied in both that history and the modern State of Israel. Yet, despite all the displacement and suffering, the settlers of this land continue to be friendly and welcoming.

Traditional fishing boats in the old harbour at the ancient city of Akko (Acre) on the north coast.

A BRIEF HISTORY

The land we know today as Israel has had many names during its history. In ancient times it was Canaan and Pilistia (coastal land of the Philistines), then Israel and Judea, before reverting to Palestine (the name ultimately derived from the Philistines). In 1948 the modern State of Israel was proclaimed.

Early Times

Cave dwellers were the earliest inhabitants of the region, especially in the Carmel (Haifa) area. The first real settlements, founded in the Late Stone Age (c.7500 B.C.–4000 B.C.), included the world's oldest walled town, Jericho. This was also the time when people started rearing animals, irrigating the land, and making pottery. By the Early Bronze Age (c.3200 B.C.–2200 B.C.), people had begun fortifying their towns, building temples and palaces, and founding the first city-states.

It was also the time when the region was the homeland of the Canaanites and other tribes familiar from the Bible, which is still the best source of knowledge about ancient Israel. It tells us that Abraham made a covenant with God which called for his descendants to conquer many lands. So Abraham, the first Patriarch, led his nomadic group of Israelites from Mesopotamia to the mountains of Canaan, where they fought the ruling Egyptians. Eventually famine compelled Abraham's tribes to move into Egypt and into captivity. In about 1250 B.C., Moses, the Israelites' new leader, parted the Red Sea and led his people back to Canaan to confront the Philistines, who now controlled much of the land. Moses died on the journey to the Promised Land, but Joshua took over from him, and between 1400 B.C. and 1000 B.C. the tribes of Israel conquered all the lands north and south of Jerusalem, most famously bringing

HISTORICAL LANDMARKS

c.1800 B.C. Abraham leads Israelites from Mesopotamia to Canaan, but famine forces them to Egypt and slavery.

c.1250 B.C. Moses and Joshua lead Exodus from Egypt back to the Promised Land, bringing down the walls of Jericho.

c.1004–928 B.C. David and Solomon reign during Golden Age.

c.721 B.C. Assyrian invasion scatters the Israelites, who subsequently wander the world as the Ten Lost Tribes.

587 B.C. Babylonians force Israelites into exile and slavery.

63 B.C. Romans conquer Palestine; Herod made King of Judea.

5/6 B.C.–A.D. 38/9 The life and teachings of Jesus.

A.D. 331 Constantine legalizes Christianity; develops Holy Land.

638 Muslim forces conquer Middle East and Jerusalem.

1099 First Crusade drives Muslims and Jews from Jerusalem.

1187 Saladin regains Jerusalem and Palestine for Muslims.

1517 Ottomans overrun Middle East, staying four centuries.

1918 Britain given League of Nations mandate over Palestine.

1933 Thousands of Jews flee to Palestine from Nazi Europe.

1948 British withdraw and the State of Israel is declared, almost immediately resulting in the first Arab-Israeli War.

1956 Suez Crisis precipitates Sinai War with Egypt.

1967 Israel defeats its Arab neighbours in Six-Day War.

1973 Israel wins Yom Kippur War against Egypt and Syria.

1978 Camp David Peace treaty drawn up with Egypt.

1982 Lebanon War, resulting in Israeli-Lebanese security zone.

1987 Intifada (Palestinian Arabs uprising) begins in Gaza.

1990–91 Gulf War; Haifa and Tel Aviv struck by Iraqi missiles.

1993 Israeli government gives PLO self-rule in Gaza and Jericho.

1994 Israel signs treaty with Jordan; borders are opened.

1995 In November prime minister Yitzhak Rabin is assassinated; Benjamin Netanyahu later becomes prime minister.

1998 50th anniversary of Israel's founding celebrated.

the walls of Old Jericho tumbling down with the sounds of their horns. At this time only the northern area was known as Israel; the south was called Judah. In its Greek form, Judea, it was applied to just Jerusalem and its immediate surroundings.

In about 1023 B.C., the chiefs of the tribes of Israel elected Saul to be their first king. David, the son of Jesse, later became king and conquered Jerusalem, the last undefeated place in the whole territory, and made it his Royal City. He also strengthened the city and brought in the Ark of the Covenant (holding the Ten Commandments) to sanctify it as a holy city and to unite the tribes. His kingdom prospered, and by the time his son Solomon succeeded him, in about 965 B.C., almost all the extensive, rich lands between the rivers Nile and the Euphrates were part of the Kingdom of Israel.

King Solomon ruled during the Golden Age of Jerusalem and is remembered for his wisdom, for the construction of the

The oasis of Jericho, and rock drawings in King Solomon's Timna copper mines (left).

First Temple, and for his copper mines in the south. After 37 years of rule, Solomon died and the kingdom was split between the northern and southern tribes. In about 721 B.C., the north (Israel) was invaded and devastated by Assyrians. The tribes of Israel were then scattered to roam the world as the Ten Lost Tribes. Even more devastating was the 587 B.C. invasion by the Nebuchadnezzar-led Babylonians. Jerusalem was razed, the Temple destroyed, and its people forced into exile and slavery.

By the fourth century B.C. the Babylonians had been overthrown, and the Israelites returned to their land, which was now under the more tolerant rule of the Persians. The Persians were followed by Alexander the Great, after whom came two Greek generals Seleucus and Ptolemy, who brought Hellenistic control to the Eastern Mediterranean for some two centuries. Around A.D. 141, the three Maccabee brothers overthrew the Seleucids and established their own Hasmonean dynasty and an extensive empire which dominated Palestine as far as the Golan in the north and Gaza in the south.

Romans and Christians

The Roman invasion of Palestine in 63 B.C. swept aside Jewish resistance, and in 40 B.C. Herod the Great, whose engineering feats and brutality became legendary, was installed as the King of Judea.

Jesus was born in Bethlehem in 6 or 5 B.C. (his birth was miscalculated in the sixth century), though it was only in the final three years of his life and ministry that his teachings became a major problem for Jerusalem's rulers. Ironically, Jesus was condemned not by the Romans, but by the Sanhedrin, the supreme Jewish legislative court, largely because of his "blasphemous" declaration that he was the Son of God. After his crucifixion, the rather precarious balance of Jewish government under Roman rule turned to revolt in A.D. 66,

The archangel Gabriel suddenly appears to Mary in the town of Nazareth.

when the Zealots took Jerusalem. They held it for only four years, but the city was razed once again (just as Jesus had prophesied), the fortress of Masada fell, and the Jews were again taken into exile and slavery. Jewish culture nonetheless survived the second destruction of the Temple. Its centre moved to Tiberias in the Galilee.

In A.D. 331, Constantine, the Roman emperor, legalised Christianity and together with his mother, Helen, developed and excavated Christian sites. Pilgrim interest in the Holy Land (as it was first called at this time) began on a massive scale that has continued to this day. Thus began a period of prosperity which was only brought to a violent end in 614 when Persian armies invaded. Once again Judea was conquered by foreign forces and Jerusalem reduced to rubble.

Arabs and Crusaders

In 622 Islam was born, according to the teachings of the prophet Mohammed. Islamic armies swiftly conquered the whole of the Middle East. By 638 they controlled Palestine, and with the construction of the Dome of the Rock and the El-Aksa Mosque in Jerusalem this became the third-holiest of all Muslim cities (after Mecca and Medina).

Muslim rule was largely tolerant, and continued peacefully for nearly four centuries with a joint Christian-Muslim protectorate of Holy Places. In 1009, however, churches were destroyed by the fanatical *Caliph* (Arab ruler) Hakim, and in 1071 Seljuk Turks took over Jerusalem and began attacking Christian pilgrims. The Pope called on Christian Europe to launch a Crusade to defend the Holy Land, and in 1099, under the command of Godfrey de Bouillon, the Crusaders took Jerusalem. Their brutality was legendary; Jews fared no better than Muslims and were massacred as "God killers." The Crusaders set up their own kingdom in Jerusalem and began another Crusade to gain more of the Holy Land. They managed to control much of the country for nearly a century before the Muslim leader Saladin (Salah-ad-Din) defeated them in 1187. A year later, Richard the Lionheart, one of the leaders of the Third Crusade, won back Akko (Acre) but failed to regain Jerusalem. Other Crusades followed, but the knights never recovered their earlier territories, and by the end of the 13th century were faced with a new enemy.

Mamelukes to Zionism

Akko fell to the Egyptian Mamelukes (freed slaves of Turkish/Circassian origin) in 1291, bringing to an end the Crusader period. The Mamelukes ruled Palestine for two hundred years, leaving behind some very fine architecture.

In 1516, the Turkish Ottoman dynasty conquered the whole of Jerusalem and the Holy Land, extending their Middle-Eastern empire. Their second sultan, Suleiman (the

King David's Tower, a mighty bastion built by Suleiman the Magnificent in the 16th century.

Magnificent), is renowned for constructing new walls and gates and roughly re-shaping the Old City of Jerusalem into its modern form. During his reign Palestine flourished, but his successors proved less able, and over the next four centuries the country continuously declined to become a virtual backwater.

In the last decades of the 19th century, many thousands of Jews of the Diaspora seeking refuge from persecution immigrated to Palestine. In 1878 the first modern Jewish colony was founded at Rosh Pina, and in 1896 Theodore Herzl, the founder of the Zionism movement that called for the creation of a Jewish State in Palestine, published his seminal work, *The Jewish State*.

The British Mandate

Around the turn of the century Britain and other countries had noted with great interest the developments in Palestine, and during World War I the British courted Jews and Arabs for help to get rid of the Ottoman Empire. They promised to the one a national Jewish homeland and to the other protection of their rights, as set out in the 1917 Balfour Declaration.

The Ottoman Empire surrendered when World War I ended the following year, and, following a declaration by the League of Nations (the forerunner to the United Nations), Britain became rulers of Palestine by mandate. A massive inflow of Jewish immigrants from around the world followed, increasing tension between Arab and Jew. In spite of British attempts to appease both sides, Arab attacks on Jewish settlers became common, Jews retaliated, and the British imposed restrictions on Jewish immigration. A Jewish underground resistance force (Irgun) was set up to fight the British and smuggle more Jews into Israel.

In the 1930s, persecution of European Jews forced even greater numbers to flee to the Holy Land. Palestinian ports, such as Haifa, were blockaded by the British to prevent more Jewish immigrants from flooding in. World War II forced the Jewish people into an alliance with the British against the common Nazi enemy. Even so, by 1947 immigration had swollen the Jewish population to such an extent that Jews now outnumbered Arabs three to one (600,000 to 200,000), and the violence continued to escalate. Unable to solve "the Palestinian problem," the British presented it to the United Nations, whose solution was to partition the country into two territories. According to this plan, areas that were predominantly Arab — the Gaza Strip, the central part of the country, the northwest corner, and the West Bank — were to remain under Arab control as Palestine, while the southern Negev Desert and the northern coastal strip would form the new State of Israel. Jerusalem, the most fiercely disputed real-estate, came under international protection.

The State of Israel

On 14 May 1948 the British Mandate ended and the State of Israel was proclaimed. Immediately the first Israel-Arab war erupted, with the new state engaged in fighting the combined armies of Egypt, Jordan, Iraq, Lebanon, and Syria. After a year of war the UN interceded to broker a peace agreement. Israel's boundaries were redrawn and expanded to almost what they are now, whereas the Palestinian Arab territories were reduced to the central-eastern area, known as the West Bank (of the Jordan River), and the Gaza Strip. Jerusalem was divided into east and west, under the control of Jordan and Israel respectively.

Jewish settlers still flooded into Israel, and new settlements continued to be built. But the young state was soon engaged in another crisis with an Arab neighbour. Gamal Nasser's nationalization of the Suez Canal international waters triggered a combined Israeli-French and British attack on Egypt, and the start of the Sinai War. The outcome was further territorial gains for Israel with control of the Sinai and the Gaza Strip. However, strong international pressure forced Israel to withdraw — with Egypt reclaiming the Sinai and a UN force installed in the Gaza Strip.

No fewer than eleven years passed before the next major Arab-Israeli conflict flared. As Arab armies massed on the borders of Israel in 1967, the Israeli Air Force destroyed the air forces of Egypt, Syria, Jordan, and Iraq with a preemptive strike. The war was over in six days. Israel gained total control of Palestine, including Jerusalem, Gaza, and the West Bank, as well as Egypt's Sinai and Syria's Golan Heights.

Piety shown at the Western Wall, or Wailing Wall.

A symbol of Israel—defiance at Masada.

Attempting to regain the Sinai and the Golan, Egypt and Syria struck back at Israel in 1973, on the holiest day of the Jewish year, Yom Kippur. Israel was caught off guard but held out on the Syrian front for over a month. Finally, peace was agreed, with a UN buffer zone created in Golan Heights.

Egypt and Israel made an important movement towards a permanent peace between an Arab nation and Israel when they agreed to a treaty in 1978. Yet, further military action lay four years away. The Israeli army invaded southern Lebanon in 1982 to safeguard its northern border against attack by the Palestine Liberation Organization. Israeli forces then penetrated north to bombard PLO positions in Beirut. They forced the PLO out, but without much support within Israel.

Intifada to the Present

A fatal road incident in the Gaza Strip in December 1987 set off the Palestinian *intifada* (uprising) against the Israeli troops in the Occupied Territories. Stone throwing and petrol bombing were early weapons, but subsequently the Palestinian Fundamentalist movement Hamas took to other forms of anti-Jewish violence, such as the 1994 suicide bombing of a Tel Aviv bus which resulted in the death of 22 people.

More traumatic to the hard-bitten Israelis was the launching of Scud missiles at Tel Aviv and Haifa during the Gulf War of 1990–91. Little physical damage was inflicted, but the psychological effect was significant. The Israelis couldn't even retaliate, being restrained by pressure from the American government, which wanted to preserve the Arab alliance against Iraq.

The most dramatic recent changes in the relationship between Arab and Jew became public in 1993 when the Oslo peace accord was finally made between former enemies, the PLO (acknowledged representative of the Palestinian people) and the Israeli government. The accord allowed Jericho and the Gaza Strip a limited form of self-government under the auspices of the PLO. Another bout of progress occurred in 1994 when a peace agreement was signed with Jordan, leading to the opening of the southern Eilat-Aqaba and Arava border routes. In November 1994 the PLO leader Yasser Arafat, the Israeli prime minister Yitzhak Rabin, and his foreign minister Shimon Peres jointly accepted the Nobel Peace Prize in celebration of their considerable achievements.

One year later Rabin was assassinated. His successor, Benjamin Netanyahu, an American-educated conservative, has slowed the implementation of the Oslo accord.

The peace process is fragile; the Gaza Strip is still given to unrest and the Israeli government watches cautiously to see if Yasser Arafat's PLO can effectively police its allotted territories, free of the influence of Hamas and Islamic Jihad ("Holy War," an Islamic fundamentalist movement). The Palestinian Arabs are irritated by Israeli land seizures. For visitors the peace dividend is currently considerable, allowing access to the number of great sights that lie in the Sinai and Jordan, including the fabulous city of Petra.

WHERE TO GO

Israel is a small country, measuring just 445 km (260 miles) north to south and 112 km (70 miles) at its widest point, yet it packs in so many sights that you couldn't possibly see them all in the space of a two-week or even three-week trip.

Jerusalem is the undisputed star attraction of Israel. And within easy travelling distance of the city are the other major sights of the Dead Sea region. If the city bustle and noise become tiresome, or you simply cannot face another religious site, try a week in the south (Eilat) or in the north (Galilee and Golan). It could be the tonic you need.

Don't try to get around all regions in one trip, however, or you will short-change them all by not having enough time to really appreciate the scenery and lifestyle.

JERUSALEM

The Old City

The historic walled heart of Jerusalem dates back beyond the time of Christ. It's intensely atmospheric, satisfying even the most demanding expectations of visitors.

Tombs with a view — the sacred Jewish cemetery on the Mount of Olives, Jerusalem.

Start by the **Jaffa Gate,** one of eight entrances that punctuate the towering city walls built mainly by Suleiman the Magnificent in the 16th century, though some parts date back more than 2,000 years.

The landmark tower just to the right, inside the Jaffa Gate, is the **Citadel** or **King David's Tower,** also built by Suleiman. Beautifully restored and with lush archaeological gardens, its towers and rooms now house an impressive state-of-the-art museum encompassing the history of Jerusalem, and offering a perfect introduction to the Old City. In the summer, you can enjoy the dazzling sound and light shows that are staged on Monday, Wednesday, and Saturday evenings.

Diagonally opposite Jaffa Gate is the narrow entrance to **David Street,** the main thoroughfare of the Old City. Here begin the *souqs* (the traditional markets) and your first taste of the old Jerusalem—with its narrow, cramped alleys, dimly lit by bare bulbs, bustling with exotically-dressed peoples of many nationalities. Show even the merest interest in any of the shops and you'll be warmly welcomed, indeed sometimes dragged inside!

Temple Mount

At the far end of David Street, **Temple Mount** is one of the world's most sacred spots to three major religions. It was here, on the hill known as Mount Moriah, that Solomon created the First Temple in 964–957 B.C. as home to the Ark of the Covenant. It was destroyed by Nebuchadnezzar in 586 B.C. and replaced by the Second Temple in 525–520 B.C. This was enlarged by Herod, sacked in A.D. 70, and totally flattened by Emperor Hadrian in A.D. 135. Temple Mount is now a large stone-paved platform, an oasis of tranquillity and well-deserving of its Arab name *Haram ash-Sharif,* the

HIGHLIGHTS OF ISRAEL

Akko (Acre). This charming port and old Crusader capital still echoes with memories of the knights of old, while the fine El-Jezzar Mosque, the Citadel, and *caravanserais* feature among the visible legacies of its Muslim conquerors. (See page 56)

Caesarea. Here are the finest Roman remains in the Holy Land, in an unsurpassed beach and coast setting. (See page 51)

Coral World, Eilat. Enjoy the magical coral and fish kaleidoscope of the Red Sea, by walking under the water, or going one better with snorkel and mask, or diving if you can. (See page 76)

Masada. The views from this clifftop eyrie are exhilarating, and listening to the story of its defenders *in situ* makes for a moving experience. (See page 70)

Mount of Olives, Jerusalem. The view of Jerusalem is unforgettable; below are beautiful churches, the Garden of Gethsemane, and Mary's Tomb. (See page 33)

Old City, Jerusalem. This is the pulsating heart of the Holy Land, with highlights ranging from Temple Mount's Dome of the Rock and exquisite Muslim architecture (to the east) to the adjacent Western Wall, and generally home to an extraordinary number of Christendom's holiest places—as well as noisy, crowded *souqs*. (See page 21)

Petra. Jordan's famous "rose-red city" lives up to its reputation. Perfectly preserved, it remains a truly magical sight. (See page 77)

Sea of Galilee. These peaceful hills and valleys have changed little in two millennia. The view from the Church of the Beatitudes may well count as a highlight of any trip to Israel. (See page 62)

Timna National Park, near Eilat. This natural wonderland of strangely eroded blood-red rocks is a major feature of excursions south into the extraordinary Negev Desert. (See page 74)

Noble Courtyard. For admission to its two great mosques buy a ticket at the booth by the foot of the steps. Note that photography is not allowed.

Standing at the centre of Temple Mount is Jerusalem's greatest architectural achievement, the **Dome of the Rock,** whose golden cupola is the city's most famous landmark. Built in A.D. 688–691, it is decorated in thousands of exquisite, predominantly blue and yellow, Persian ceramic tiles, with Koranic scriptures on the lintels. Looking up at the interior of the great dome is just as breathtaking as seeing it from outside. On the mosque floor rests a huge ancient slab, the Rock itself, on which Abraham prepared to sacrifice his son Isaac (but was given a last-minute reprieve by an angel) and from which the prophet Mohammed rose to Heaven during his dream-visit to Jerusalem. You can still see Mohammed's footprint, but you'll need a guide to point it out.

Mohammed also visited the **El-Aksa Mosque,** which is adjacent to the Dome mosque. El-Aksa is actually the most important mosque in the entire city. The present silver-domed building largely dates from 1034, but the original mosque

---

Holy Relics and Legends

As well as Mohammed's footprint, the Rock is apparently marked with the fingerprints of the archangel Gabriel, who held the rock down while Mohammed ascended, and the footprint of Enoch. A few strands of Mohammed's beard may also be seen, carefully displayed in a wooden cabinet next to the Rock.

According to the Jewish Talmud, the Rock covers the mouth of an abyss in which the waters of the Great Flood can still be heard roaring. Muslim tradition has it that the Rock is hovering (quite unsupported) and that below it is the Well of Souls, where the deceased assemble, twice weekly, to pray.

was built in 715. This too is a splendid place, hung with magnificent chandeliers, laid with priceless carpets, and decorated with fine mosaics, but you should visit El-Aksa before the Dome of the Rock, as it is bound to suffer by comparison.

Your admission ticket also allows you entry to a fascinating small **Islamic Museum.** Take your time poring over the other sites of Temple Mount, which contains some fantastic medieval fountains, arches, and gateways.

The Western Wall

Just below Temple Mount is the legendary Western Wall (*Ha-Kotel Ha-Ma'aravi* in Hebrew), better known as the "Wailing Wall." To reach the entrance, go back up David Street and turn left up a small alleyway. Airport-style security checks leave you in no doubt as to the importance of the site. A remnant of the second century A.D. wall that once supported the Temple Mount, this is the most revered place in the world for the Jewish faith. Since the sacking of the Temple and their banishment in A.D. 70, Jews from all over the world have come here to weep and wail at the loss of the House of God and pray for the restitution of Jerusalem to the Jewish people.

Whatever your beliefs, the giant stone wall is an awesome sight. Men pray to the left, women and children to the right. Prayers can be scribbled on paper and inserted into the cracks between the great stone *ashlars*

The Western Wall, at a site holy since King Solomon's time, where Jews grieve for the lost Temple.

(blocks). Gentiles may also approach; simply don the skull cap or shawl provided.

The Jewish Quarter

Immediately west of the Wall lies the Jewish Quarter. After the claustrophobic rough and tumble of the dimly-lit medieval *souqs,* stepping into this area is like entering an oasis of light, space, cleanliness, and tranquillity. The area has been razed many times, most recently during the 1948 War, so it's not surprising that most things here are modern. From David Street head into the recently excavated Cardo, the main thoroughfare of Roman and Byzantine Jerusalem and a former Crusader marketplace. Nowadays it is bordered by ancient columns and lined with expensive shops.

Nearby is the **Old Yishuv Court Museum,** where you can experience something of 19th-century Jewish life in the city through restored living quarters, kitchens, and prayer areas. The **Herodian Quarter Museum,** in the remains of six mansions which somehow survived the destruction of A.D. 70 and now lie several feet below the surface of the present city, gives a fascinating insight into life in the city 2,000 years ago.

One of the most memorable sights of the Quarter is the graceful arch of the defunct **Hurva Synagogue,** most recently destroyed in 1948 and left unrestored in memory of the area's turbulent history.

The Via Dolorosa

Head back into the chaos and noise of the *souqs* and turn right off David Street, either into the El Wad Road or along the more colourful Souq el Attarin into the long Souq Khan es Zeit, where butchers and food vendors make for fascinating window shopping. Either street will lead you along to Christianity's most melancholy thoroughfare, the Via Do-

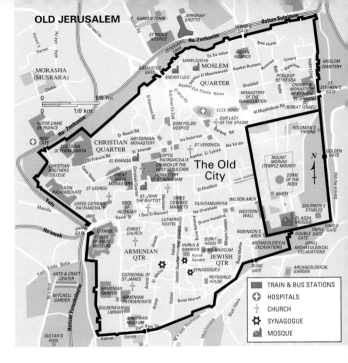

lorosa (Street of Sorrows). Here thousands of Christian pilgrims walk in the final footsteps of Jesus as he made his way to Calvary, many bearing a cross to express their piety.

Many of the 14 **Stations of the Cross,** the marked points which show Jesus's progress along the street, are highly disputed. Some can be matched with places and events in the Gospels; a few are certainly the stuff of legend, mapped out in the 16th century by European Christians who had never been to Jerusalem. As these "false stations" gained credence with pilgrims, the Franciscan monks living in the area decided that faith could be served by accommodating the fabrications, and so legend was allowed to became "reality."

Station I: Here Jesus is condemned in Herod the Great's Antonia Fortress. However, there is nothing to see, as the site is overlain by modern buildings.

Station II: Here Jesus receives the cross, is taken away, beaten, and mocked by a crowd in the fortress courtyard. Much of the actual courtyard pavement (*lithostrotos*) survives in the **Monastery of the Flagellation,** where Jesus Christ was scourged, and in the adjacent **Convent of the Sisters of Zion.** Both buildings are open to visitors. Here too you'll find the **Ecce Homo Arch,** built in A.D. 135. The name ("Behold the Man") echoes the words of the Roman prefect Pontius Pilate.

Station III: Jesus falls. There is nothing in the Gospels about this, though a **Polish Chapel,** with a relief showing Jesus bowing under the weight of the cross, marks the spot.

Station IV: Jesus meets his mother. A small **shrine** and a relief mark this poignant point.

Station V: It is from here that Simon carries the cross. A 19th-century **Franciscan oratory** is now on the site.

Station VI: Veronica wipes Jesus's face. The **Church of St. Veronica** stands on the site.

Station VII: At this point Jesus falls again.

Station VIII: It is from here that Jesus consoles the women of Jerusalem and tells them to weep for themselves and their children, rather than for him, thus prophesying the impending destruction of Jerusalem. A **cross** in stone relief now marks the site.

Station IX: Jesus falls for a third time. This is the most curiously located of the stations, in the **Ethiopian Convent** on the roof of the Church of the Holy Sepulchre. The monks of the convent are often happy to show you around their rooms.

Church of the Holy Sepulchre

The final five stations are in this strange and sacred building, which is actually five churches in one, each closely administered by one of five denominations: Roman Catholic, Armenian Orthodox, Greek Orthodox, Abyssinian Coptic, and Syrian Orthodox (demarcation lines are drawn on the floors and even on some of the pillars). This bulky fortress-like church dates mainly from the Crusader period of the 12th century. The interior is a heady mix of Crusader and Byzantine styles, and because of inter-denominational bickering, false partitions, and poor maintenance it is difficult to understand without a guide.

Following in Jesus Christ's footsteps is a popular Christian tradition on the Via Dolorosa.

Comings and goings at the Damascus Gate—the starting point of East Jerusalem.

Go up the stairs to the right of the entrance to see the next four stations. **Station X:** Jesus is stripped; **Station XI:** Jesus is nailed on to the cross; and **Station XII:** Jesus dies on the cross. The hole beneath the altar is traditionally considered the exact spot where the cross was erected (see page 32). **Station XIII:** Jesus is taken down from the cross, the point being marked by a small shrine, with an ancient wooden figure of Mary in a glass case.

Station XIV: This is the Holy Sepulchre itself, now reduced to the simple stone shelf on which the body of Jesus lay. You view it from an *aedicule* (a highly decorated, though very sombre, kiosk) holding six people at a time. The idea of enclosing it in this bizarre fashion came from a 19th-century Orthodox architect.

The Muslim Quarter

One of the most charming and peaceful Christian sites in Jerusalem, the **Church of St. Anne** (mother of the Virgin Mary) is actually in the Muslim Quarter, and just inside St.

Stephen's Gate at the far end of the Via Dolorosa. This stern, solid structure, built in the 12th century, is the finest Crusader church in the city. A chapel in the crypt marks the birthplace of the Virgin Mary. Adjacent is the impressively deep **Pool of Bethesda,** where Jesus cured the crippled man with the famous words "Stand up, take your mat and walk" (John 5:2-9). The lowest level of the pool dates back to the eighth century B.C.

The two main streets of this quarter are the El Wad Road and the Souq Khan es Zeit (see Via Dolorosa, page 26), both of which meet at the **Damascus Gate.** This is the finest of all the city gates, dating mainly from the 16th-century reign of Suleiman the Magnificent. It is also the busiest, with a steady stream of Muslims travelling in from their homes in East Jerusalem to shop and work in the Old City. A further exotic touch is added by the Muslim ladies just inside the gate, selling brightly coloured cloth and clothes, alongside street vendors selling fruits, bread, and other wares.

Archaeological excavations have revealed the great depths of the Pool of Bethesda.

East Jerusalem

East Jerusalem is mainly Arab territory and you will see few, if any, Jews in the vicinity — though visitors should not be put off. From the Old City, East Jerusalem starts at the Damascus Gate. Ironically, just a few yards from here, in the midst of all the Arab hub-

This breathtaking view of the Old City is seen from the Ramparts Walk between the Jaffa and Damascus gates.

bub and bustle, you'll find a famous, marvellously peaceful Christian site.

A little way along the busy Nablus Road a sign on the right points to the **Garden Tomb.** It was General Gordon (of Khartoum fame) who in the late 19th century popularized the idea that this was the true site of Jesus's burial. Calvary and Golgotha both mean "skull" and there's certainly a pronounced skull-shape to the adjacent hill. As the British Protestant guardians of the tomb modestly inform you on a free guided tour, there is much evidence that this, rather than the Church of the Holy Sepulchre, is the place where Jesus was crucified and buried. Whatever conclusion you may reach, this beautifully laid-out garden, containing a typical rock-hewn cave tomb of the first century A.D., is a highlight of many pilgrimages.

Farther along the Nablus Road, the sturdy, square, handsome tower of **St. George's Cathedral,** which was consecrated in 1910, is a little piece of England in the heart of Arab Jerusalem. A few yards on, at the heart of the American Colony established by American missionaries in the late

19th century, is the **American Colony Hotel,** a mansion built in the style of a Turkish fortress in 1860. The American mission was based here around the turn of the century. It is famous as a place of tolerance where Arabs and Jews can meet without enmity.

On the main road, alongside the walls close to the Damascus Gate, you will find **Solomon's Quarries,** which are also known as Zedekiah's Cave after a legend that King Zedekiah and his army fled from the Babylonians via this route in 587 B.C. These atmospheric red caves stretch several hundred yards back beneath the Old City, and it isn't difficult to imagine the slaves of King Solomon quarrying stone by candlelight to build the Second Temple. Follow the city walls a little farther along until you come to the landmark **Rockefeller Museum,** built in 1927, which contains the city's finest collection of archaeological artefacts.

The Mount of Olives

The best way to visit the Mount of Olives is to start at the top and work your way down. From the Damascus Gate (see page 31) take either a shared taxi (*sherut*) or a bus 42 or 75 to get to the Seven Arches Hotel. The view from the promenade here is arguably the finest in the city; go in the morning, when the sun is at your back, for the best photographs, or go in the

---

Walking the Ramparts

For a bird's-eye view of the Old City take the Ramparts Walk between the Jaffa Gate and the Damascus Gate (other sections may be open according to the political situation). The best views are from near the Damascus Gate. The views as you walk closer to the Jaffa Gate are obscured by tall buildings. Note that women are not advised to take this walk at night.

evening for the sunset. Immediately below is the most sacred Jewish cemetery in the world. Jewish tradition has it that on the day of the Second Coming the Messiah will descend here to resurrect the dead, who will then follow him through the Gate of Mercy (the now-blocked Golden Gate, directly below the Dome of the Rock from here) into Jerusalem.

Just down the path on the right, you will find the 1955 Franciscan **Church of Dominus Flevit** ("The Lord Wept") marking the spot where Jesus wept as he predicted the destruction of Jerusalem (Luke 19:41-4). Just below this lies the **Tomb of the Prophets,** believed to be the burial place of Haggai, Malachi, and Zechariah. The tomb guardian will unlock the gate to the tunnel and give you a candle to explore the small circular catacomb, but for what little you can see, it is hardly worth the effort.

Go back up to the main promenade road, turn left, and you will find two more sites associated with Jesus. The **Church of the Pater Noster** is where he is said to have taught the dis-

The White-Russian Orthodox Church of Mary Magdalene is rarely open, but the exterior alone is a lovely sight.

ciples the Lord's Prayer, and around the cloisters of the adjoining convent there are tiled panels bearing the famous words in almost every world language. Adjacent is the **Chapel/Mosque of the Ascension,** located on the spot where Jesus is believed to have begun his ascent to heaven. This is actually a Muslim place of worship

The poignant Garden of Gethsemane at the foot of the Mount of Olives.

(Muslims recognise Jesus as a prophet, though not as the Son of God). A rather damaged footprint, purportedly that of Jesus, is on display.

Follow the steep road right down the hill, and on your left you will soon see the highly picturesque **White-Russian Orthodox Church of Mary Magdalene.** The great attraction of the church is the splendid exterior, which is crowned by golden onion-shaped cupolas. However, the church is only open on Tuesday and Thursday (10:00 A.M. to 11:30 A.M.).

Beyond this, to the right, is **Mary's Tomb.** A fine Crusader arch leads down a dimly-lit broad stairway to the dark subterranean **Church of the Assumption,** a Greek Orthodox church. The recess on the right half-way down contains the tombs of the Virgin's parents, Anne and Joachim; the one on the right is the tomb of Joseph. At the bottom of the stairs, encircled by dozens of smoky, scented votive lamps, a rockhewn sepulchre marks the tomb of the Virgin (though this is also claimed by the Church of the Dormition, see page 37). Turn left out of Mary's Tomb to the adjacent **Franciscan Grotto,** which is thought to have been used by Jesus while teaching his disciples.

The legendary Tomb of Absalom — the son of King David of Israel — and the Tomb of Zechariah.

A short way along the busy main road is the **Garden of Gethsemane.** This charming, peaceful spot, where Jesus grieved, prayed, was betrayed by Judas, and arrested by the Roman soldiers, takes its name from the ancient olive trees (*geth-shemna* means oil-press) which have been grown here since before Christ's time.

Alongside the garden, the **Church of All Nations** is best seen in the afternoon when the sun's rays bounce off the brilliant mosaic façade. Built in 1924 and funded by many nations, it contains the rock at which Jesus is said to have prayed the night before he entered the city of Jerusalem for the Passover supper.

Cross the road to a track leading down into the **Kidron Valley,** immediately below the Old City walls. Here are three fine first-century B.C. tomb monuments. The finest is the huge conical-roofed **Tomb/Pillar of Absalom** (King David's son). Nearby, with a pyramidal roof, is the impressive **Tomb of Zechariah** (though it's unclear whether this is Zechariah the prophet or Zechariah the father of John the

Baptist). The third tomb, which belongs to the **Bene Hezir,** is the only one to have been authenticated. This is also the place where the disciple James is said to have hidden, following the arrest of Jesus by the Romans.

Mount Zion

Despite its romantic name Mount Zion is actually little more than a hill immediately south of the Old City walls. Its great landmark is the **Church/Abbey of the Dormition.** Its name, meaning "to sleep," comes from the legend that the Virgin Mary spent her last earthly days here before she "fell asleep." Consecrated in 1908, the church is a handsome Neo-Romanesque structure with a relatively small, bright, modern interior. Follow the stairs at the right of the entrance to the room where the Virgin Mary slept.

Behind the church are two more sites of great religious significance. In a tiny low-ceilinged room, draped with blue velvet, is the revered but questionable **Tomb of King David.** In the same building is a small, humble, vaulted room, called the **Coenaculum** ("dining hall"). It is here that Jesus is said to have washed the disciples' feet and presided over the Last Supper. The Crusaders built the Gothic archwork in the 12th century; it was rebuilt in its present form in the 14th century.

Zion

The word Zion, meaning "City of David," appears in the Old Testament as a title for Jerusalem, and is also synonymous with Israel. Mount Zion was the site of the ancient city captured by King David (II Samuel 5:6-9), and God dwelt on Zion, from where he protected the Children of Israel (Joel 3:16). Zionism is the name of the movement dedicated to reestablishing a Jewish homeland in Palestine (see page 16).

Finally, on Mount Zion, you will find the **Chamber of the Holocaust,** an eerie, candle-lit place with disturbing images and grim reminders of the horrors of Nazism.

West Jerusalem

West Jerusalem is a general name for the area west of the Old City. It is thoroughly Jewish, almost entirely modern, and still growing.

The New City

The heart of the New City is around **Kikkar Zion** (Zion Square), where shops, restaurants, and hotels are great attractions for tourists and locals alike. The most attractive enclave is the pedestrianized precinct centred on Ben Yehuda Street and Yoel Salomon Street. Formerly the Nahalat Shivia residential district, founded in 1869 and restored in 1988, the

---

Jewish Enclaves

If you're looking for that old-time European *shtetl* (ghetto) feel, then schlep along to **Mea Shea'rim,** a ten-minute walk from Jaffa Gate or Damascus Gate. This small rundown area is the last surviving community of its kind in the world. There are no sights as such, but lots of people dressed in the antiquated ultra-Orthodox Chassidic (mid-18th-century Polish) garb of long black coats, white shirts (no ties), black trousers or breeches, and white knee-length socks, topped off with a black broad-rimmed hat. Dress conservatively and behave respectfully.

A more modern, though equally traditional, Jewish atmosphere can be experienced at the **Mahane Yehuda** fresh-produce market along the Jaffa Road (catch any bus going towards the station along this road). It's best on Thursday and Friday before sunset—just enjoy the hustle and bustle.

area is characterized by small golden-stone courtyard houses, many converted to restaurants, cafés, and arts and craft shops. More shops can be found on Ben Yehuda Street, King George V Street, and Jaffa Street.

Yemin Moshe

Just south of the New City and immediately west of the Old City is the exclusive residential suburb of Yemin Moshe, named after Sir Moses Montefiore (1784–1885), a famous Anglo-Jewish philanthropist. The best-known building here is the **King David Hotel,** built in 1930, and now a solid, aristocratic home-away-from-home for kings, presidents, and other well-heeled visitors (see page 132). Directly opposite is another famous landmark, the **YMCA Building** (built in 1928–1933), with a very handsome Art-Nouveau tower (see page 133).

The focal point of Yemin Moshe is the elegant white-washed **Windmill,** erected by Sir Moses in 1858–1860 to help feed the first residents here. A small display inside is dedicated to the benefactor. There are a number of other minor attractions in this grassy park area: **Herod's Family Tomb;** a fine replica of Philadelphia's **Liberty Bell;** and a modern **Lion Fountain.** Just below here you'll find the **Cinematheque** (see pages 90 and 140).

The Israel Museum and Farther West

Take buses 9, 17, or 24 for the short journey west to the finest museum in the country, the **Israel Museum.** It's a large complex, focusing mainly on archaeology, arts of the world, and Jewish art. Many of the exhibits are of international standing and all are beautifully displayed and well-captioned.

The most striking part of the museum is the **Shrine of The Book,** whose gleaming white conical structure represents the shape of the lid of the jars in which were discovered the world's oldest biblical manuscripts, the Dead Sea Scrolls (see page 68). The imaginative display of the actual scrolls inside should answer all your questions. The excellent Youth Wing of the museum for children and teenagers is opposite.

To get your bearings take the free daily Museum Highlights Tour and/or pick up the leaflet *A Quick General Tour.*

Directly opposite is the **Bible Lands Museum.** It's too much to do this and the Israel Museum in a day, but students of Middle Eastern history should definitely return.

A five-minute walk away is Israel's Parliament, the **Knesset.** The modern building wins few admirers, but there is a free tour (Sunday and Thursday, 8:30 A.M. to 2:30 P.M.) and you can watch the debates (Monday through Wednesday, 4:00 to 7:00 P.M.). Passports needed for both. Tapestries by Chagall and mosaic floors are the interior highlights.

Another site within walking distance is the beautiful, ancient walled **Monastery of the Cross,** now hemmed in by suburbs. Built by 11th-century Gregorian monks, it stands on the site of the tree from which the True Cross was made.

Farther to the west (buses 13, 17, 18, 20, 23, 24, 26, 27) lies one of the world's saddest memorials. **Yad Vashem**—it means "a monument and a name (which shall not perish)"— is Israel's Holocaust Museum complex. It tells the story of the Holocaust in words, pictures, art, sculpture, and other exhibits. It is imaginative, dignified, often harrowing, deeply moving, and essential viewing to get an historical perspective of modern Israel. Entrance to the museum complex is free.

THE WEST BANK

Many Jews still use the evocative biblical names of Judea and Samaria, but to the rest of the world this area is much better known as the West Bank (or the Occupied Territories, though this term is unacceptable to many Israelis). The designation of the name came about after the land west of the Jordan River was annexed by Jordan in 1950. Recaptured by Israel in 1967, it has become synonymous with the struggle between Jewish settlers and Palestinian Arabs, each fearful of the other encroaching onto what they perceive as their rightful territories.

The West Bank is in political limbo. Only a few years ago it would have been dangerous for visitors to travel anywhere within the region. Today official tourist-office advice still tends to be cautious; many areas are relatively safe for independent travel, though it is vital to keep abreast of daily news and best to avoid potential flashpoints such as Nablus and Hebron. Gaza, on the Mediterranean coast, is most troubled of all and is best avoided altogether. The safest way to travel in the West Bank is as a new member of an Arab-led tour group. Cars with Israeli license plates (including rented cars) are often targets of violent attacks.

Little seems to have changed in the streets of the
"little town of Bethlehem."

Bethlehem

The "little town of Bethlehem" is a Palestinian settlement where Christians worship and Jews trace the line of David. Not surprisingly, therefore, it is one of the Holy Land's many religious hot-spots. There are two main sights here. The first, which lies on the main road from Jerusalem, is **Rachel's Tomb,** revered by all three religions of the Holy Land (Rachel was the wife of Jacob and died here while giving birth to Benjamin). It is a very simple, low-key site, housed in a small 19th-century building.

The heart of Bethlehem is **Manger Square,** now a car park ringed by souvenir shops and packed with street hawkers. Everyone who comes visits the fortress-like structure of the **Church of the Nativity.** Imposing but not beautiful, it is not only the oldest church in the Holy Land, but also one of the oldest in the world. First built in A.D. 325 by Constantine, it was remodelled two centuries later by Justinian, and again by the Crusaders in the 12th century. The entrance is through a tiny sixth-century doorway, so low you have to bend almost double. This may have been to stop soldiers on horseback storming into the church. The dark and atmospheric basilica is divided into five naves, with a floor made from stone and

More West Bank Monasteries

The monasteries at **Wadi Quelt,** 3 km (2 miles) west of Jericho, and **Mar Saba,** 19 km (12 miles) southeast of Jerusalem, are worth visiting if the political situation allows. Both on ancient sites, they were rebuilt in the 19th century and hang precariously on their valley edges. St. George at Wadi Qelt is the most impressive monastery in Israel, set amidst a surrounding area also offering superb hiking.

wood. Trapdoors swing back to reveal original mosaics, while gilded lamps hang from the oaken ceiling. Like the Holy Sepulchre in Jerusalem, this church is too important to stay in the hands of one denomination, so it is administered jointly by Greek Orthodox, Armenian, and Franciscan priests.

The Monastery of the Temptation, perched precariously on a mountainside near Jericho.

The Altar of the Nativity just about drips with gold and silver. To the side of the choir pilgrims queue to descend to the **Grotto of the Manger,** a simple marble-clad niche in the cave wall that is lit by an array of hanging lamps. A blackened 14-pointed silver star marks the birthplace of Jesus.

Minor sights include the **Milk Grotto,** where Mary is said to have hidden with Jesus before the flight to Egypt, and the **Shepherds' Fields,** where biblical flocks were supposedly watched by night.

Herodian

For spectacular views of both Bethlehem and Jerusalem, and for countryside straight out of the Bible, take a trip 10 km (6 miles) southeast to Herodian. This hill fort was built by Herod the Great (74–4 B.C.), whose misdeeds were so enormous that he felt he needed a bolt-hole closer to Jerusalem than Masada (see page 70) to protect him from his many enemies. Between 24 B.C. and 15 B.C., he had a small natural hill carved into an impregnable 100-metre- (300-foot-) high artificial mini-mountain, capped by a mighty fortress and palace. The site is still compelling, though the fort itself is ruined.

Jericho

Jericho, one of the most famous names in antiquity, is the oldest walled town in the world. Radio-carbon dating on the lowest portions of the walls (sent tumbling by the horns of Joshua in 1200 B.C.—Joshua 6:20) indicates that there was a settlement of some 3,000 people at this spot as long ago as 7800 B.C.

There is little for visitors in the modern Arab centre. The remains of the ancient city, **Tel Jericho,** are on the northern edge of town. Legendary associations aside, however, even this site is of minor interest, except to archaeology buffs. Look northwest from here and you will see a much more impressive sight in the distance. **The Monastery of the Temptation,** said to be on the spot where Jesus was tempted by the Devil for 40 days and nights, clings to the mountainside. Built in 1874, it houses some very fine icons.

Jericho's other main attraction is the ruin of **Hisham's Winter Palace,** located 2½ km (1½ miles) northeast of town. Used as a hunting lodge by the seventh- and eighth-century Muslim Ummayad dynasty, from what little remains, including some excellent mosaics, it is obvious that it must have been palatial.

TEL AVIV AND JAFFA

Tel Aviv is in many ways the epitome of the New Israel dream. The city that has become second in size only to Jerusalem began as recently as 1906 as a tiny neighbour to the noisy, crowded Arab town of Jaffa. The settlement burgeoned, and it soon became evident that this was no mere garden suburb, but a major new city. Indeed, it was to become the first new Jewish city for 2,000 years. Over a million people now crowd into Greater Tel Aviv and its

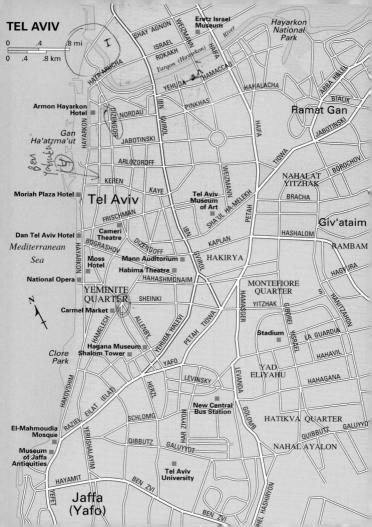

This striking Tel Aviv apartment building is a modern structure in the most modern of Jewish cities.

surrounding "satellite towns." Old Jaffa has become the quiet neighbour.

The city was built in a hurry, with little planning or control, and so has few parks or open spaces and only limited architectural character or charm. It does have a certain polyglot big-city style, however, and it is a major centre for culture, business, fashion, and nightlife, with some superb museums as well as an attractive beach. Old Jaffa, on the other hand, is worth a day of anybody's time.

Central Tel Aviv

If you want an overview of Tel Aviv, take the lift to the 35th floor of the **Shalom Tower** (132 metres/433 feet), formerly the tallest structure in the Middle East (a communication tower in the military base near the Tel Aviv museum of Art recently surpassed it). Just to the west is the beach, obscured by serried ranks of huge high-rise hotels on Ha-Yarkon Street. The beach, which runs all the way to Jaffa, has soft, golden sand, best tended near the hotels. At weekends and holidays it is packed and is the place to be seen.

Parallel with the north end of the beach is Tel Aviv's busiest thoroughfare, **Dizengoff Street.** A good place to stroll and people-watch, it has many of the city's busiest and most important shopping, eating, and drinking places. Dizengoff Circle's bizarre multi-colour cog-wheel fountain, known as *Water and Fire,* has the same sort of magnetic appeal for people as London's Piccadilly Circus. Every hour on the hour from 11:00 A.M. to 10:00 P.M. it revolves to music, the water dances, and it emits a jet of flame.

Just north of the Shalom Tower is the **Yemenite Quarter,** its main attractions being the bustling Carmel market and good Oriental restaurants. Nearby, the **Hagana Museum** tells the fascinating story of underground Zionist activity in the run-up to independence.

The modern concrete-and-glass structure of the **Tel Aviv Museum of Art** houses an excellent collection of Israeli and

What's in a Name?

A *tel* is an artificial mound created on the accumulated debris of the past (generally associated with such ancient sites as Megiddo or Jericho). Tel Aviv was not constructed on an ancient site, but had already started building on top of itself when it was named. Its full name means "Hill of Spring," symbolizing hope for the future.

Jaffa is Yafo in Hebrew, which may well be derived from *yafah/yofi* (beautiful) or may simply come from the name of its founder, Japhet, son of Noah.

European art spanning the 16th to 20th centuries. One of its features is a notable Impressionist Gallery. The museum is well laid out and the perfect size for relaxing away a couple of hours on a wet day.

Tel Aviv University Museums

To the north of the city, on the Tel Aviv University campus, lie two more excellent museums. The more conventional of the two is **Eretz Israel** (the Land of Israel), spread out over small pavilions which deal with conventional museum subjects such as coins, glass, philately, ceramics, ethnography, folklore, etc. In addition there is an artisan's workplace, and you can visit archaeological sites still under excavation.

The Beth Hatefutsoth, or **Museum of the Diaspora** (the Diaspora relates to the dispersal of the Jewish people worldwide), is quite possibly the finest museum in Israel and certainly the most innovative, yet it doesn't contain a single exhibit of any age. Instead of ancient artefacts it shows the lifestyle and achievements of myriad Jewish communities around the globe through high-tech audio-visual displays, hands-on exhibits, scale models (many of which are exquisite), and reconstructions.

Buses 13, 24, 25, 27, 74, and 79 serve both museums, though you wouldn't have the energy to see both in a day. In addition, buses 45 and 572 serve the Diaspora Museum and bus 89 will take you to the Eretz Israel Museum.

Jaffa

In stark contrast to the 20th-century metropolis of Tel Aviv, and a mere 30-minute walk away, Jaffa is one of the oldest cities in the world and almost certainly the oldest port still in use. It was from here that Jonah boarded the ship for Tarshish in his attempt to flee the instructions of God (Jonah: 1, 3), only to be swallowed by the whale. Greek mythology also has it that Andromeda, the beautiful daughter of the King of Jaffa, was chained to a rock at sea just outside the harbour, as a sacrifice to a sea monster (but she was rescued just in time by Perseus).

Jaffa has been courted, crushed, and rebuilt by a succession of conquerors, from the ancient Egyptians to the Ottoman Turks. **Old Jaffa,** the heart of the city, on a hill overlooking the port, was last refurbished in 1963, and today has a thriv-

Jaffa's historic port is still a colourful place after more than 2,000 years.

ing artists' colony as well as various tourist shops, restaurants, and nightspots. For some people it's become a little too gentrified, but the port below still has something of a salty, working atmosphere.

The best way to learn about Old Jaffa is to join a free guided walking tour each Wednesday morning (meet at 9:30 A.M. by the landmark **Clock Tower** on Yefet Street). The centre is small and compact, perfect for strolling. A few yards uphill from the Clock Tower, turn right and you will see the **el-Mahmoudia Mosque,** built in 1812. Return to Yefet Street and continue up to the **Jaffa Flea Market,** a crowded, covered Aladdin's Cave of shiny goods and trinkets (closed Saturday). Keep on going along Yefet Street and then turn right and go down Pasteur Street to the port. The restored houses of the artists' colony lie in the maze of alleyways to the right. Turn right and you will find yourself in **Kedumin Square,** which is marked by the handsome **Church of St. Peter.** This is the heart of Old Jaffa. In the middle of the square there is an underground **Visitors' Centre** exhibiting a fascinating history of the town through excavations and lively display panels. From here you can then walk uphill to the right, to the pretty hilltop gardens for a superb **view** of Tel Aviv. A little way down, in front of the hill, is the **Museum of Jaffa Antiquities.** Return to Kedumin Square and make your way down to the picturesque **fishing port** by way of the ancient, narrow honey-coloured alleyways. At the port you'll find working fishing boats, excursion boats, a marina, and fish restaurants. Go in the early evening and enjoy Jaffa's famous sunset.

THE COASTAL STRIP

With the possible exception of Tel Aviv, Israel is not known for its Mediterranean beaches, yet between the Gaza Strip in the south and Rosh Hanikra in the north there are 190 km (118 miles) of good sandy coastline. About half of it, however, is out of bounds to all but the military, but that still leaves huge areas of sand and surf. The northern coast is the most attractive region, being characterized by bays, capes, valleys, islands, and peninsulas. South of Caesarea the coastline changes dramatically and becomes almost straight, just as it appears on maps.

The beach at Tel Aviv — the sun is shining but the black flag means no swimming today.

Caesarea

The ancient city of Caesarea is the jewel of the Coastal Strip, an extensive, dramatically excavated archaeological site and an attractive beach resort rolled into one. The first Caesarea, built in 22–10 b.c., is said to have been Herod's attempt to rival the pomp and splendour of the ports of Alexandria and Athens. Creating a city boasting a major harbour, including a 500-metre- (1,640-foot-) long breakwater, with little more than soft sand as a base, was undoubtedly a colossal feat of engineering. Caesarea became the largest city in Judea, its chief port, and home to the governor and to Pontius Pilate. It was the Tel Aviv of its day — loud and licentious, the place where it all happened. Caesarea lived, and died, to the full. In the First Jewish War (A.D. 66–70), many thousands of Jews were massacred here, and thousands more died later in the Roman amphitheatre here in the name of entertainment. This was where the disciples were confronted by the Holy Ghost, and St. Paul was imprisoned in the city for as long as two years.

The Arabs captured Caesarea from the Byzantines in A.D. 639 and the Crusaders conquered the Arabs in 1101,

---

Diamonds

Israel has never mined a diamond, but it is a major centre for cutting and polishing. Call in at the **Netanya Diamond Centre** on Benjamin Boulevard in Netanya (see page 52), to see the work in progress and admire its glittering end product. There is also a model South African diamond mine, a gem museum, and short film. Of course there is a shop, but there's no heavy pressure to buy — browsing rather than buying is the norm here.

discovering a green crystal vessel which they claimed to be the Holy Grail, the cup from which Jesus and his disciples drank during the Last Supper (it now reposes in Genoa). The city was conquered and reconquered for 200 years before being destroyed by Muslim armies in the 13th century. Ancient Caesarea disappeared from history, only to be uncovered in the 1940s.

The most notable remains of the ancient city are the massive **Roman aqueduct,** the **Roman hippodrome,** the **amphitheatre** (which is now used for classical music concerts) and a fourth-century **synagogue.** You can eat and shop in and around the once-magnificent and heavily fortified **Crusader city,** with its enormous ramparts and cathedral. Modern Caesarea boasts a couple of high-quality beachside hotels, a handful of other accommodations, some pleasant restaurants, a country club, and the only 18-hole golf course in the country. The beach, right beside the Roman aqueduct, is particularly charming.

Other Resort Towns

There are three other resorts along the strip, used almost exclusively by Israeli citizens. **Ashkelon** is a site of great antiquity (perhaps 4,000 years old). Samson had his famous haircut here, but he would find it hard to recognize the thoroughly modern town of today.

Herzliya, which was named after Theodore Herzl, the founder of modern Zionism, is Israel's most upmarket resort, with superb beaches and high prices, but nothing of historical or sightseeing interest.

Prosperous **Netanya** has a large expatriate English community, excellent beaches, a fine park, and low cliffs which form an attractive backdrop and keep the hotels from encroaching onto the sand. It is also the capital of the Sharon

Plain citrus-growing area and the centre of Israel's diamond industry (see page 51).

HAIFA AND THE NORTHERN COAST

This northwest corner of Israel has been relatively unexplored by tourists, yet it holds some of the country's finest sights, including the third-largest city, modern Haifa, and the Crusader town of Akko, better known as Acre.

Haifa

Hilly Haifa drapes itself dramatically over the slopes of Mount Carmel. The city had a fairly nondescript history until this century, when the construction of the Haifa-Damascus railway and the massive new harbour (finished in 1934) transformed it into the vital trading and communications centre it is today. It became a focus of Jewish-British confrontation just after World War II as Jewish immigrants tried to run the British blockade (see page 17), and became the first major city under Jewish control at the end of the British Mandate in 1948. Today, it is a busy industrial city with the country's only metro service, the Carmelit subway. This subterranean funicular shuttles from the port to the residential district in just six minutes.

Beach/Port Area

Haifa has a number of good beaches, just to the west of the port in the Bat-Galim area.

Nearby, the fine **National Maritime Museum** in Allenby Street charts 5,000 years of Red Sea and Mediterranean seafaring, while the **Clandestine Immigration and Naval Museum** documents the defiance of the British blockade to smuggle immigrants into Israel. On the other side of the road is **Elijah's Cave,** a venerable spot where Elijah hid from the irate King Ahab after wiping out his religion (see page 56.) Also, the Holy Family are said to have sheltered here on their return from Egypt.

From here, a steep path and stairs lead 800 metres (2184 feet) up an age-old pilgrims' path to the **Stella Maris Carmelite Church and Monastery,** built in 1836 over a cave also believed to have been inhabited by the prophet Elijah. Alternatively, take one of the bulbous black **cable cars** which make the ascent from the end of the Bat-Galim promenade.

If you can bear the thunderous traffic, the area around the Place de Paris Carmelit terminus is a good earthy place to explore, with a street market and several interesting small shops and eating houses. The enormous 68-metre (223-foot) **Dagon Grain Silo,** by the port, is still working, but opens for tours (Sunday through Friday, 10:30 A.M.) and contains a museum. The **Haifa Railway Museum,** on Hativat Golani Road, has a number of large locomotives and exhibits to please any train-spotter.

The Carmelite Church, nestled a steep 800 metres up an ancient pilgrim's path.

Hadar Area

Haifa's most famous attraction is the splendid golden-domed **Baha'i Shrine and Gardens** (entrance on Zionism Avenue; Shrine open daily 9:00 A.M. to noon, gardens open daily 8:00 A.M to 5:00 P.M.), the international headquarters of the 4-million-strong Baha'i faith, which was founded by the Persian holy man, Baha'u'llah (who died in 1892). The movement believes in universal peace, brotherhood, and charity, and incorporates elements of all the major religions, accepting Buddha, Moses, Jesus, and Mohammed as prophets. The Shrine, completed in 1953, is also the tomb of the Bab, the forerunner of Baha'u'llah. It is surrounded by luxuriant formal gardens with marvellous views. The gardens are being extended in a massive $200 million project designed to include even more magnificent hanging gardens.

The Baha'i Shrine, headquarters of the 4-million-strong Baha'i faith, overlooks the Hadar area below.

Just up the hill from here is the bucolic Mitzpe Ha-Shalom, also called **Peace View Park,** containing a peaceful sculpture garden, and also offering splendid views.

For the **Haifa Museum,** take the Carmelit subway to Ha-Nevi'im, and walk along Shabtai Levi Street. The museum has ancient and modern art, an excellent archaeology section, and temporary exhibits of music and ethnology.

Central Carmel

Carmel Man, a relation of the Neanderthal family, lived here 600,000 years ago. Carmel is now an elegant residential and hotel district (Carmelit to Gan Ha-em) featuring the best shops, restaurants, and cafés. Most visitors stay up here and stroll at night along the charming **Louis Promenade,** by the big hotels, to enjoy the vast, spectacular panorama of Haifa's lights glittering below.

Other places of interest are the **Mane Katz Museum,** Yefe Nof Street, the **Prehistory Museum and Zoo,** Ha-Tishbi Street, and the **Ruben and Edith Hecht Museum of Archaeology,** on the Haifa University campus at Mount Carmel.

Druse Villages

Southeast of Haifa (bus 1), the pleasant villages of **Dalait el-Carmel** and **Isfiya** are occupied by the Druse, a sectarian Muslim group who reject many of the teachings of Islam and share very few allegiances with the Palestinian Arabs. There's not a great deal to see but the markets and shops are good for souvenir hunting, and you'll find that the hospitable Druse make the visit very enjoyable.

About a five-minute drive south stands the **Muhraka Carmelite Monastery,** on the spot where Elijah, with the help of Yaweh (God), defeated the Ba'al god in a test of spontaneous combustion, leading to the death of 450 heathen priests. Stunning views extend from this peaceful monastery, which is open daily 8:00 A.M. to 1:30 P.M. and 2:30 to 5:00 P.M. (closed Friday afternoon).

☛ Akko (Acre)

An important ancient Phoenician, Greek, and Egyptian city long before the arrival of the Arabs and Crusaders, Akko is one of the most rewarding places to visit in Israel. It has the colour and vitality of an old Arab town, but little of the usual hassle, boasting superb Crusader and *caravanserai* buildings, a fine mosque, and a picturesque port. This is all within a few blocks, interwoven with narrow ancient streets.

The **Mosque of El-Jezzar,** built in 1781, dominates the landside of the old city (the other three sides jut into the

The streets of Old Akko are ideal for just wandering about and soaking up the atmosphere.

Mediterranean). El-Jezzar ("the butcher") was a brutal Albanian pirate who became *pasha* (the Ottoman regional governor) during the late 18th century and was responsible for building much of the surviving Old City. His mosque is the third largest in Israel and the most important outside Jerusalem. Visitors are welcome from early morning until 12:30 P.M., then for a few hours in the afternoon (enquire at the tourist office).

Almost opposite the mosque gate are the tourist office and the entrance to the **Crusader City,** which was buried by El-Jezzar, who simply constructed his new citadel on top of the Crusader structures in order to avoid dismantling their enormous foundations.

The First Crusade to recover Palestine reached its climax here in 1099, and Acre became the Crusaders' capital and a key port in their struggles for the Holy Land. Only a small part of their city has been excavated for fear that further work may cause the whole town to collapse. Nonetheless, enough is open to get a very good feel for its grandeur and enormity. As there is little interpretation inside, try to see the introductory film first (showing throughout the day from 9:00 A.M. to 5:00 P.M.). Your ticket also entitles you to visit the **Municipal Museum,** which is actually no more than a well-preserved late-18th-century *hammam* (Turkish bath).

Browse through the Arab **market** behind the mosque and wander the alleyways towards the port. You will pass some of Akko's four *khans* or *caravanserais*—inns with large inner courtyards used by travellers and their caravans. The 18th-century **Khan el-Umdan** (Inn of the Pillars) is the finest. It's near the port; its clocktower is a famous landmark.

The old fishing **port** is a bustling, colourful hubbub of activity, from where you can take excursions or hire your own boat in summer.

Continue round the city seawalls to the northernmost corner and you will come to the entrance to the **Citadel.** This imposing structure, built by El-Jezzar (see page 57), nowadays holds the **Museum of the Underground Prisoners,** which documents the Jewish resistance movement that fought against the British during the Mandate period (part of the film *Exodus* was shot here). It's an interesting account of the violent history of modern Israel, and ends in the Scaffold Room where nine Jews were executed. The highlight of the Citadel is the rooftop view over the El-Jezzar Mosque.

Leave the city by its eastern Nikanor Gate for a five-minute walk to **Hof Argaman** (Purple Beach), one of Israel's finest beaches. There is a fee, but the facilities are good.

St. Peter's Fish

The Sea of Galilee is famous for this local fish which St. Peter and the other disciples would no doubt have caught and eaten. It's said that the distinctive "finger-marks" by its gills were left by Peter as he picked up the fish.

The Sea of Galilee is a favourite spot for pilgrims and sightseers.

Nahariya and Rosh Hanikra

Nahariya is a quiet beach resort with fine white sands and good leisure facilities. Rosh Hanikra, near the Lebanese border, is famous for its dramatic sea grottoes embedded in the white chalk cliffs and reached by cable car.

THE GALILEE

The Galilee is Israel's lushest landscape, with grassy slopes, fertile valleys, and, to the north, rolling hills and majestic mountains. Above all, HaGalil (as Galilee is known in Hebrew) is associated with Jesus, who based his short ministry here and performed eight of his eleven most famous miracles on and around the Sea of Galilee. This area is not just for pilgrims, however; it is also for those in search of the great outdoors, whether for sports activities or simply hiking.

Nazareth

The place where Jesus grew up, Nazareth, is today a small, dusty Christian Arab town with sprawling modern developments swamping the old town and ancient sights. Its enormous, ornate churches are a far cry from the simple biblical sites of the imagination. The main sights are not obvious, so call in at the tourist office on Casa Nova Street for a free guide map.

The centre of attention is the huge **Basilica of the Annunciation,** standing on the traditional site of the Virgin Mary's house and the cave where the archangel Gabriel appeared to Mary to herald the birth of Jesus (Luke 1: 26-31). Built in 1966, it is a stunningly modern building that polarizes opinion. In parts its interior resembles an airport concourse more than a conventional church. At the heart of the new church, however, are the remains of churches from the fourth, fifth, and 12th centuries. Unless you're a lover of this type of architecture, the highlight will probably be the many colourful, inventive murals donated by different countries, depicting the Virgin and Child, often quite unashamedly in their own national image.

The First Kibbutz

Some 8 km (5 miles) southeast of Tiberias, close to where the Jordan River flows from the Sea of Galilee, is the oldest kibbutz in Israel, **Deganya Alef,** founded in 1910. A kibbutz is a collective settlement, originally agricultural in nature, though most now have some light industry (Deganya Alef boasts a thriving diamond tool factory). Many kibbutzim have turned to tourist accommodation for extra revenue.

A burnt-out tank stopped with a home-made grenade is still on display at Deganya Alef as a battle trophy of the 1948 War. The kibbutz's most famous son (and Israel's most successful modern general), Moshe Dayan, was born here in 1915. There is also a museum, the Beit Gordon, open to the public.

On the other side of the square, **St. Joseph's Church** was built in 1914 over a cave once thought to be Joseph's carpentry shop. Here too are remnants of an older church. The other main churches are all within a short walking distance. The **Greek-Catholic Church** in the centre of the animated market is the site of the synagogue where Jesus is said to have preached as a young man. Up the hill are **Mary's Well** and the handsome **Church of St. Gabriel,** on the spot where the Greek Orthodox Church believes that Gabriel appeared to Mary. Built in the late 17th or early 18th century, it is lined with exquisite paintings, wall hangings, and tiled mosaics. Other churches are scattered across the town.

Megiddo

Megiddo looms large in Christian apocalyptic beliefs, since the Bible gives it as the site of Armageddon—in the Book of Revelation, the "last battle"—which actually takes its name from the town. This may be less of a prophecy than a reflection on the town's tumultuous history. Being a vital strategic point in the trade routes between Egypt and Syria, it was fought over, razed, and rebuilt so many times from the period of ancient Mesopotamia onwards that its name became synonymous with war and destruction. It was here that British forces defeated the Turks during World War I, an event so crucial that the British commander, General Allenby, chose the title Lord Allenby of Megiddo on his elevation to the peerage.

It still has an immensely impressive ninth-century-B.C. water system, with a 65-metre- (215-foot-) long tunnel some 37 metres (120 feet) underground. It burrows from inside the city to a spring outside the walls; you can descend the steps and climb right into it. A small museum near the archaeological site explains the many layers of excavations (up to 21 metres/70 feet deep).

The Sea of Galilee (Lake Kinneret)

This historically renowned freshwater lake, known both as the Sea of Galilee and Lake Kinneret (meaning "a harp," after its shape), is just 58 km (36 miles) in circumference. The main sights are to the north of Tiberias, but it doesn't take long to get right around it.

Tiberias

Tiberias is the only settlement of any size on the lake, a modern, rather characterless resort town with high-class hotels and a lively summer nightlife. Having curative hot springs, it was founded as a spa in A.D. 18, and named after the Roman Emperor, Tiberius.

A free walking tour departs every Saturday at 10:00 A.M. from the Plaza Hotel and points out the town's historic sights, most notably the tombs of prominent rabbis. The town has a long and important Jewish heritage, as it was here, from the third century onwards, that the Mishnah (part of the Talmud, edicts of Jewish Law) was codified, the Jerusalem Talmud (the primary source of Jewish religious law) was edited, and the Hebrew alpha-

The Italian Church on the Mount of Beatitudes has the best view over the lake.

bet developed. The Sanhedrin, the great court of scholars and rabbis, also met here, and Tiberias became one of Israel's four holy Jewish cities, along with Jerusalem, Hebron, and Safed. For many, however, the highlight of a visit to Tiberias is to relax with a drink on the **lakeside promenade.**

Taking the waters in a slightly different sense: there are two hot springs to choose from in the town. **The Galilee Experience** at the marina provides a 35-minute audio-visual introduction to the region; **pleasure cruisers** run to Capernaeum and other places; and you can also hire small craft.

Around the Lake

The **Church of the Multiplication of the Loaves and Fishes,** at Tabgha, marks the site of one of the most famous miracles of all, in which Jesus is said to have fed the 5,000 with five loaves and two fishes (Mark 6:36-45). The present church, built in 1982, is a pleasant, light and airy building with a famous fifth-century mosaic floor, depicting among other things a basket of bread and two fishes.

One of the high spots of a tour around the lake, both literally and metaphorically, is the **Mount of the Beatitudes.** It was on this hill that Jesus gave his famous Sermon on the Mount (Matthew 5:2-12) and also chose his disciples. Today a beautiful black-and-white octagonal church stands on the Mount, built (incongruously, with the aid of Mussolini) in 1937 and known as the **Italian Church.** The views are incomparable and the garden setting is exquisitely serene.

During the time of Jesus, **Capernaeum** was an important town located between rival kingdoms. It was the home of Peter the fisherman, his brother Andrew, and perhaps three other disciples. Christ conducted much of his ministry around here. Today there is little to see, apart from the remains of **Peter's House** (the veracity of which can neither be proved nor dis-

proved) and a ruined second-to third-century synagogue.

Nearby, in a tranquil orchard on the lake shore, stands a tiny picture-postcard **Greek Orthodox church** with white walls and brilliant red domes.

Hammat Gader

Hammat Gader is a good place for those in search of Roman remains, for those who wish to take the waters, and for children. The Roman baths are still impressive with several large bathing areas, though the hot curative waters have been diverted to a modern pool and spa.

An unusual splash of color and bit of Greece on the shores of the Sea of Galilee.

Here you can soak peacefully, slap on black Tiberias mud, be massaged by water jets, and seek solace in radioactive sulphur springs.

The **alligator farm** here is something of a curiosity. Crocodiles have lived in this region ever since biblical times, but these swamp creatures were recently imported to the area from the Florida Everglades. Waterslides and trampolines are also provided for children (at a safe distance from the formidable alligators).

Safed

Perched on a steep slope, high in the Galilean hills, Safed (known also as Tzfat, Tsfat, Sefat, and Zefat) is a delightful village-town of some 22,000 people. In summer its cooler clime makes it a favourite retreat; later in the year clouds and mists can all but obscure it—though even this has a certain charm. Safed is famous for Jewish mysticism and its artistic community, and is therefore a favourite place for coach-tour operators and independent travellers alike.

Although settled by Jews since the time of the Second Temple, the town really grew with the influx of Sephardic Jews fleeing the Spanish Inquisition. In the 16th century it reached its zenith as the centre of Kabbalism, a form of Jewish mysticism, and boasts 21 synagogues, a seminary, and 18 schools. Some of Judaism's most important and influential rabbis are buried here.

The town is basically divided into three areas. The upper part, the **Park,** contains the scant remains of a **Crusader castle,** from where there are spectacular views on a clear day. This area is bounded by Safed's principal thoroughfare, **Jerusalem Street,** which becomes a traffic-free promenade in the centre of town, with small shops, restaurants, and cafés. Pick up a map from the tourist office here and ask about walking tours. On the way, look out for the preponderance of two colours: blue (symbolizing God's reign as King of the world) and green (symbolizing the growth of redemption). From Jerusalem Street, a flight of steep steps, known as **Ma'alot Olei Hagardom Street,** leads downhill. At the bottom, turn left for the **Artists' Quarter,** where you will find numerous artists' studios and galleries. The greatest concentrations are in the General Exhibition Hall and along Arlozorof Street, though you will find top-quality art in galleries and studios throughout the lower town. Turn right and head for the **Old City/Synagogue Quarter.** Only two synagogues, the **Ha'Ari** and the **Caro,** are of real note. Nearby is a fascinating Ethiopian Folk Art Centre.

What makes Safed special, however, is being able to simply enjoy strolling the ancient, narrow cobbled alleyways.

The Golan Heights

The Golan Heights, with their commanding views over the surrounding lands, have always been strategically vital. The current dispute over the Golan is merely perpetuating a tradition that goes back to the ancient Romans.

Syrian territory before 1967—when Israel seized it in the Six-Day War, then annexed it by parliament decree in 1981 —the Golan isn't recognized as Israeli territory by the United Nations, but as an Occupied Territory. A UN buffer zone separates the protagonists.

The sightseeing highlight of the Golan is **Banias,** scenically situated on the southern slope of Mount Hermon. It is famous for being one of the main sources of the Jordan River, and the waterfall near Metulla lies close to the actual spring (where

The Jordan River

This holy river, famous from the stories in the Bible, is the largest and most important water source in the country. It has three tributaries: Nahal Hermon, Nahal Dan, originating from a spring at the foot of Mount Hermon (see page 66), and Nahal Senir, originating in Lebanon. The three join in the Hula Valley to become the Jordan and flow into the northern part of the Sea of Galilee, providing its main water source.

The Jordan just east of Jericho is where Jesus was baptised by John the Baptist. This holy site has been closed to the general public for some years. However, Roman Catholics may visit on one day in October, while the Greek Orthodoxy make a pilgrimage at Epiphany. Contact the Christian Information Centre at Jaffa Gate in Jerusalem for more details.

you can swim). This natural force has been venerated by man since early times, as shown by the cave-temple of Pan, to whom the Syrians and Greeks dedicated the stream. Herod also dedicated a temple here to his patron, Augustus Caesar, and, symbolically, Jesus came to this hotbed of "false religion" to

Dead Sea luxury—an inviting pool at En Boqeq on the southern shore.

reveal his true identity to the disciple Simon Peter (Matthew 16:13). A small Greek Orthodox church commemorates the event. The Muslims continued the tradition of worship, substituting the "green prophet" Elijah for Pan; and the Crusaders built a town here, very little of which remains. They also erected a fortress, called **Nimrod's Castle,** on the site of a structure supposedly built by the same man who built the Tower of Babel. The area was also home to the extremist Muslim Hashishi sect, whose cut-throat violence introduced the words "assassin" and "hashish" into the English language.

THE DEAD SEA

A visit to Israel would not be complete without a trip into the Judean Desert to the Dead Sea, which forms part of the border between Israel and Jordan. The Judean Desert is the lowest point on earth at 400 metres (1,312 feet) below sea level. The Dead Sea (actually a lake) is fed mainly by the Jordan River and flash floods, but because the land is so low the water has no outlet. In the shimmering heat of the desert the water continually evaporates, leaving behind strangely-shaped salt formations and water with a mineral content some 30 percent more concentrated than ordinary sea water.

Mud, mud, glorious mud—and there's nothing quite like the Dead Sea variety.

No animal, fish, or plant life can live in these waters, but the human body can float like a cork on the surface.

Qumran

The Dead Sea is synonymous with the Dead Sea Scrolls, ancient rolls of writing in Hebrew and Aramaic. These were first found accidentally by a Bedouin goatherder in 1947, in caves at Qumran, 2 km (1 mile) from the northern shore of the sea. The scrolls, written by the first-century B.C. Essene sect, are the earliest known biblical manuscripts in existence. They were stored in cylindrical pottery jars and kept perfectly preserved in the almost moisture-free conditions of the caves. They shed no new light on Jesus, but they are of enormous interest to scholars of the Bible, Jewish history, and the cultural environment of early Christianity.

The caves can be spotted from the roadside but are easy to miss unless a guide points them out. There is very little to see here, or at the ruined Essene monastery of Qumran itself. But the scrolls are on display in the excellent Shrine of the Book in the Israel Museum, Jerusalem (see page 39).

Ein Gedi

The name of this desert oasis on the shore of the Dead Sea means "goat's spring." If you are travelling independently, be sure not to miss the **Ein Gedi Nature Reserve,** where David's Spring waterfall will wash off the desert dust, and hyraxes and ibex leap across the rocks (get here early in summer to avoid the crowds).

If you're on a coach tour, you will probably stop at the excellent **Ein Gedi Spa** and get your chance to float on the Dead Sea. There are changing rooms and showers, sulphur pools, a beach (with curative black mud you can smear all over your body), a swimming pool, restaurant, and full health-spa facilities, including clinics and massage to tone and relax the body. Although it's not cheap (admission to in-

Dead Sea Bathing Tips

The high concentration of minerals in the Dead Sea is said to be very therapeutic, but getting it into any open cuts will be painful. Don't shave before a dip! Similarly, try not to get water in your eyes; it feels like hot gravel, so splashing and conventional swimming are out. If you do get water in your eyes, keep calm; don't rub them and the sensation will soon pass. Don't swallow the water either; it has a bitter soapy-oily taste. Once you leave the sea, have a shower to get rid of the sticky film coating your body and hair.

To get that laid-back floating feeling, just wade in. When the water is up to your thighs, sit back gently as if leaning back in your favourite armchair, then slowly stretch out your legs. Bring a copy of the *Jerusalem Post* to read.

dependent travellers is by day ticket only), this is without doubt the best place to sample the Dead Sea in comfort.

☞ Masada

The name "Masada" (meaning "fortress") is an Israeli rallying call for freedom or death. Israeli schoolchildren make the long climb to swell national pride, and army recruits are sworn in here with the words "Masada shall not fall again."

The cliff of Masada soars to 440 metres (1443 feet) above the Dead Sea and is totally isolated from the surrounding mountains by deep gorges. On top is a broad plateau 650 metres (2,132 feet) long by 300 metres (984 feet) wide. Although fortifications were built here by the Maccabees in the second century B.C., King Herod the Great improved on these hugely, transforming them into a magnificent fortified palace, stocked with years' store of food and fitted with enormous cisterns (supplied by flash floods via an aqueduct) to ensure a plentiful water supply.

Conquering Masada the easy way: it took the Romans a little longer!

In A.D. 66 Zealots (a militant Jewish organization) captured the fortress and moved in with their families. Numbers grew until eventually 967 people lived here, surviving on the vast storehouses of food and water conveniently cached by their late enemy. Initially, the Romans ignored this isolated rebel stronghold, but in A.D. 72 they laid siege with an army of some 10,000-

15,000 men, outnumbering the Zealot male fighting force by about 30 to 1.

A conventional siege was useless against such a seemingly impregnable rock, however, and with so much food and water the Zealots could not be starved into submission. Instead, the Romans built a gigantic ramp of rock and earth extending from the nearest adjacent mountain so they could simply march up to the level of the walls. Having held out for some three years, the Zealots could only watch in horror as the ramp neared completion, knowing only too well that, if taken alive, their women and children would be horribly brutalized, their men would be butchered in the ring by animals or gladiators, and the survivors would be sold as slaves. On the last night before the Romans breached the walls the Zealots decided on mass suicide. "They chose ten men from amongst them, by lot, who would slay all the rest...and when these ten had without fear slain them, they cast lots for themselves, he who was last of all set fire to the royal palace [of Herod] and ran his sword into his body." Two women and five children hid to escape the slaughter and told the story to the Roman chronicler Josephus Flavius, who recounted it in his remarkable book *The Jewish War*. Ever since then, Masada has been more or less deserted.

You can now ascend the great rock by walking up the Snake Path—a hot and tiring ascent that takes 30 to 60 minutes depending on your fitness. It's much easier, but quite expensive, to take the cable car. Once on top you can see the ruins of Herod's once-magnificent palace, the ramp that sealed the Zealots' fate, and, way down below, the sketchy remains of the Roman siege camps. It's essential that here of all places you have a good guide to bring the site and epic story to life.

Spectacular sound-and-light shows are staged at Masada in the summer.

The Negev may look forbidding and deserted, but thousands of Bedouins call it home.

THE NEGEV

The Negev (literally "the dry land") does not offer rolling vistas of sand dunes, but is instead a rocky wasteland of savage natural beauty. It covers an area of some 12,000 sq km (4,600 square miles) from Beersheba in the north to the Gulf of Eilat in the south—over half of Israel. The desert around highway 90 along the eastern border is flat, but the southernmost Arava Valley section offers striking views east to the mountains of Jordan and west to the strange pink-and-red rock formations of the Timna area. If you approach Eilat from Beersheba (via highway 40) the terrain and road are very different: slow, twisting, and undulating among myriad peaks and hills, reaching a climax at the eyrie of Mitzpe Ramon.

Beersheba

Birthplace of Isaac and Jacob, this is the only town of any size in the region (population 130,000). There is little here of any interest except the traditional **Bedouin market,** held every Thursday morning.

Mitzpe Ramon

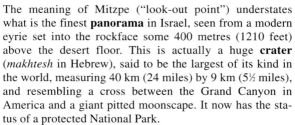

The meaning of Mitzpe ("look-out point") understates what is the finest **panorama** in Israel, seen from a modern eyrie set into the rockface some 400 metres (1210 feet) above the desert floor. This is actually a huge **crater** (*makhtesh* in Hebrew), said to be the largest of its kind in the world, measuring 40 km (24 miles) by 9 km (5½ miles), and resembling a cross between the Grand Canyon in America and a giant pitted moonscape. It now has the status of a protected National Park.

The look-out point is part of a stimulating **Visitors' Centre** which interprets the geology, geography, and fauna and flora of the region. The surrounding modern settlement of Mitzpe Ramon is the natural base for walkers who want to

---

Bedouins

50,000 Bedouins inhabit the very thinly populated Negev. Their camps are easily recognized by the square black tents and flocks of sheep, goats, and the occasional camel. But their traditional cross-border nomadic way of life has been curtailed by the Israeli authorities, and the true Bedouin lifestyle is diminishing day by day as permanent settlements become more common.

A visit to the Museum of Bedouin Culture at Kibbutz Lahav, which is 24 km (14 miles) due north of Beersheba, will reveal a great deal more about this disappearing culture.

explore the crater below. Above, you'll find an **Alpaca and Llama farm,** which offers enough attractions to make this a pleasant family outing.

To the north is the site of **Avdat,** a second/third-century B.C. Nabatean trading town on the route from Gaza to Petra (see page 77). Its Byzantine bath-house is one of the best preserved in Israel, and the views over the Negev are superb.

☛ Timna Park

The Timna area, just north of Eilat, is renowned for **King Solomon's copper mines.** Said to be the oldest of their kind in the world, dating back some six millennia, they were worked by the ancient Egyptians and later (perhaps) by King Solomon's slaves. Copper was still extracted from here until very recently. In **Timna National Park** you can see some of the 10,000 old mine shafts found here and the remains of smelting places. And you can even descend into caves to see ancient rock drawings. The best reason to visit Timna Park, however, is to see its multi-coloured sandstone rock formations, fantastically shaped by desert erosion.

A short video at the park entrance recounts some of the local history, after which you can explore seven major sites, all well-signposted, in your own car. You can drive right up to some; others require a walk. Curiosities such as the Arches and the Mushroom Rock are self-explanatory. Most spectacular of all sites is **King Solomon's Pillars,** an almost sheer rock-face towering some 50 metres (150 feet) high, shaped into huge pillar-like formations. At the base are the remains of a 14th-century-B.C. temple to the Egyptian goddess of love, Hathor, while above there are steps leading to a contemporary Egyptian inscription.

A short distance north of Timna Park is the **Hai Bar Wildlife Reserve,** where rare and endangered indigenous animals are bred for eventual release back into the wild. There's a small zoo area where you can see snakes, lizards, birds of prey, wolves, hyenas, foxes, and various desert cats, including cheetahs and leopards. Then it's off aboard the coach into the reserve's safari park to see these animals, as well as others, roaming freely.

Eilat

Eilat (pronounced *Ill-at*) is the "sun and fun capital" of Israel, a purpose-built town that has sprung up from an isolated military base to become an international holiday resort in less than 45 years. Eilat is on the Red Sea, but has a very Mediterranean feel and, like many such boom towns, isn't preoccupied with planning or architectural aesthetics. However, it enjoys an excellent geographical location (which is perfect for excursions into the Negev or across the borders to Jordan and Egypt), year-long sunshine, superb underwater sports, plenty of nightlife, and good hotels. The public beaches are slightly disappointing, but the great attraction is to be found beneath the waves,

North Beach, Eilat, with the mountains of the Negev as a backdrop.

where you can dive or snorkel among brilliantly-coloured coral and fish.

Eilat divides into three distinct areas. The **town** itself, built on a hill, features most of Eilat's shopping — much of it in large malls — several restaurants and nightspots, and an excellent tourist information office. Call in for a free map if nothing else. **North Beach,** just a ten-minute walk away, is the hotel zone, built around a marina. This also includes several restaurants and nightlife venues. The third section of Eilat, **Coral Beach,** extends for 6 km (3 miles) from North Beach, so you'll need some form of transport to get there. In between there is an unattractive stretch of coast marred by port and industrial facilities. In the same area, however, right alongside the Egyptian border, are the best beaches and the most outstanding underwater scenery in the whole country.

For a perfect introduction to Eilat's sub-aqua delights, visit **Coral World,** a fascinating complex with large tanks holding native sharks, rays, and turtles, as well as aquaria of incredibly coloured, bizarrely shaped denizens of the deep. And, best of all, there are underwater observatories sunk into the sea 90 metres (300 feet) offshore at the end of a pier so you can see what is happening in the **Coral Beach Nature Reserve.** You can explore underwater trails here, either with a snorkel or with full diving equipment. If you want to go farther out to sea without getting your feet wet, Coral World also has a state-of-the-art yellow submarine. It's a great novelty, but very expensive. Cheaper options include a floating observatory and glass-bottomed boats (all of them departing from the North Beach marina).

Nearby on Coral Beach, the excellent **Dolphin Reef** is not a conventional dolphinarium but a research centre for the study of dolphins in a natural habitat. The dolphins swim in a netted section of the sea and are occasionally taken out into the open sea for a taste of freedom. Visitors can see dolphins being trained and fed every two hours from 10:00 A.M. to 4:00 P.M. Most visitors watch from either the jetty or the observation tower, but for a bit extra you can get onto a floating plat-

A hawksbill turtle, one of the many fascinating residents at Coral World.

form with the trainers or, even better, swim with the dolphins.

Allow enough time to spend at least half a day here, and pack your swimming gear. The entrance fee allows you to use the prettiest, and the best, sandy **beach** in all of Eilat.

The **Aerodium,** behind the Sport Hotel, North Beach, is a free-fall skydiving simulator which lets you actually "fly" (with the aid of a special suit), buoyed up on a jet of air, 3–4 metres (10–12 feet) above the ground. You will receive a one-hour course, including instruction on the rudiments of flight. This is open to anyone over the age of eight in reasonable physical condition.

EXCURSIONS BEYOND ISRAEL

Petra

The fabulous "rose-red city" of **Petra** (Wadi Musa in Arabic), one of the finest sights in the Middle East, lies a mere two-hour drive from Eilat, across the border in the Jordan mountains. On the way you can also visit **Wadi Rum** (famous for its association with Lawrence of Arabia).

Perfectly preserved in a secret valley and not rediscovered until the early 19th century, the city of Petra is an enchanting place of magic, expressed through its setting and the swirling pink patterns of its rocks as much as through its dramatic architecture.

The adventure begins inauspiciously at the visitor centre near the entrance gates (this is the place to enquire about official guides). Inside the gates, dozens of horses await to transport you gently along the 2½-km (1½-mile) track through the *siq* (gorge) to the city. They are suitable for all ages and much more comfortable than walking along the hot, dusty, stony track. Entering Petra on horseback certainly feels right, particularly if you are wearing your best Indiana Jones hat (parts of *Indiana Jones and the Last Crusade* were shot here). On the way you'll see the first of the huge Nabatean tombs and the remains of Roman pavements. The *siq* walls narrow until you reach a cleft, through which you glimpse **El Khazneh** (the Treasury), and then the *siq* opens out to bring you face to face with the ancient city's most famous sight.

Like most of the structures here, the 40-metre- (120-foot-) high Treasury (named after legends of lost treasure) was hewn from the red sandstone valley sides. Beyond the façade there are cavernous empty rooms. It is thought to have been used as a temple, and dates back to around 100 B.C.

Petra may be a bit hard to get to, but well worth the trip for the amazing ruins.

Petra was largely created in the first to third centuries B.C. by the Nabateans, an Arabic tribe who grew rich from trading with (and extracting protection money from) the great caravans which passed this way. Up to 20,000 Nabateans may have once lived here, but earthquakes in the fourth and eighth centuries destroyed most of the city; what remain today are only the sturdiest, most monumental tombs and

Petra Practicalities

Take your passport (which must be valid for at least another six months) and plenty of money (dollars and/or *shekels*) and a sense of humour—border formalities can take some time. The service is comparatively new, so ask fellow travellers to recommend a good tour operator at an affordable price.

There is a significant visa fee for entering Jordan (how much depends on your passport) and a not-inconsiderable exit fee. The drive to Petra takes about two hours, and Petra itself requires at least half a day, so a night in Jordan is inevitable. The border opening times are limited and subject to change, so check with the Jordanian embassy before you go. It's best to arrange for your visa ahead of time, also, or to travel with an organized tour that will make the arrangements for you.

If you want to travel independently, you'll find you cannot take an Israeli hire-car into Jordan, and there is no public transport from the border to Petra. Either hire a taxi or arrange for a Jordanian car-hire company to bring a car to the border post from Aqaba. An alternative is to use the services of the enterprising hotels near Petra, which offer a package of accommodation and transport to and from the border. Ask the tourist office in Eilat (see page 124) for up-to-date information.

Finally, be aware that you may need to extend your personal travel insurance (before leaving home) for travel outside Israel.

temples. The Romans took control of Petra in A.D.106, and they too have left their legacy.

With the shift of trade routes from land to sea, Petra's importance declined dramatically. The last major visitors were the Crusaders. From then until 1812, when the intrepid Swiss explorer John L. Burckhardt rediscovered Petra, it was almost totally forgotten.

There's only one track, wide and dusty, leading through the Lower City, so you can't get lost, and the principal sites are obvious enough. Nonetheless, a guide is recommended, as there is no interpretation except for what the site museum provides. The track continues past the **necropolis** to an impressive **amphitheatre,** very probably carved by Nabateans, but influenced by the Romans. Directly opposite, high on the cliff face, are three magnificent, crumbling **Royal Tombs,** similar in size and style to the Treasury. The track continues down through the Lower City, past Roman remains and the ruins of a huge Byzantine church, to the museum. This is the end of the Lower City and the end of most day tours.

A 30- to 40-minute climb takes you to the most spectacular of the "High Places," **El Deir** (the Monastery), another fabulous rock-hewn monument similar to the Treasury in style, but bigger. Built at the time of the Roman occupation, it wasn't a conventional monastery, but probably was a place of great sanctity for the Nabateans.

To see more of Petra (and there are many more fascinating sites worth seeing here, though no more major set-pieces to enjoy) requires a lot of climbing, a detailed guide book, and at least another day.

Egypt is an excursion also worth considering. The pyramids are generally too far from Israel for most vacationers but the extraordinary sixth-century **Monastery of St. Catherine** on the slopes of Mount Sinai is within easy reach.

WHAT TO DO

SHOPPING

Shopping in Israel is as exotic or as straightforward as you want to make it. If you want to take home memories as well as souvenirs try the *souqs* (traditional covered markets), where bargaining is the name of the game. Alternatively, there are a number of modern malls with international names as well as many excellent local shops selling goods at fixed prices.

Traditional shop hours are Sunday through Thursday 8:00 or 8:30 A.M. to 1:00 P.M., 4:00 to 7:00 P.M., and Friday 8:00 or 8:30 A.M. to 2:00 or 3:00 P.M. Shops close for the Sabbath (Saturday) and re-open on Sunday, which is a normal business day. The Arab day of rest is Thursday/Friday, so most *souqs* will be closed then. Malls and tourist shops tend to open all hours to suit the local trade.

Where to Shop

Jerusalem has the widest range of goods and types of shop that you'll find anywhere in Israel. The Old City *souqs* offer all manner of Oriental wares (as well as much of less interest), whereas in the New City, Yoel Salomon Street and Rivlin Street are good for arts and crafts, and Ben Yehuda and surrounding streets can supply most other items.

Shopping in Jerusalem's Old City: always a fascinating experience.

Tel Aviv has lots of modern malls on and around Dizengoff Street, but if you are treasure hunting you should visit the flea market in neighbouring Old Jaffa (see page 48), which is also generally good for arts and crafts. Other places with interesting *souqs* are the Arab towns of Akko, Bethlehem, Nazareth, and the Druse villages near Haifa (see page 53).

Bargaining

If you are in search of a particular item, look in "fixed-price" shops first to get some idea of what you are likely to have to pay. However, even some of these will prove remarkably flexible if you try bargaining. To haggle successfully, pitch your opening price well below target and don't look too keen. Walking away is a good ploy if you have the time. Look elsewhere, and if you don't find the same thing more cheaply, you can always come back later.

What to Buy

Art: Israeli art, and particularly modern art, is of a very high standard. Jerusalem has some excellent outlets. The House of Quality on Hebron Road and the Jerusalem Artists' House on Shmuel Hanagid Street are the most famous; also try the New City. Safed, Jaffa, and Ein Hod (near Haifa) are the main provincial centres. The shops of the Israel Museum and the Tel Aviv Museum of Art are also good.

Olive-wood carvings, on sale at Jerusalem's Zion Gate, are a popular souvenir.

Clothing: Leather is a popular item, though rarely cheap; try Tel Aviv. Sandals are a tradition in Jerusalem's Old City, while an Arab *keffiyeh* head-dress (as modelled by Yasser Arafat) is useful for warding off desert dust and sun. Beware, however, as it may be taken to reflect a political opinion.

Dead Sea products: Bath-salts and mudpacks are the most popular Dead Sea souvenirs, though there's a huge range of other therapeutic and cosmetic goods for you to take home.

Diamonds: The National Diamond Centres in Netanya (tel. 09-862 4770) as well as Jerusalem (tel. 02-673 3770) will pick you up from your hotel and give you a free tour of the workshops, where they will offer a wide choice of goods to select from and expert advice on what you may want to buy.

Jewellery: This is a traditional Jewish craft, and the possibilities of what you can buy are almost endless. For something different, look for Roman glass jewellery or fashionable filigreed Yemenite earrings and necklaces (in Jerusalem, Jaffa, and other places that are craft-oriented). In Eilat you should look for Eilat stone, an attractive combination of malachite and azurite.

Judaica: Traditionally-crafted ceremonial objects, such as *menorahs* (a seven-branched candelabra) and *mezuhahs* (inscribed parchments/parchment holders), may not be to everyone's taste, but they are undeniably Israeli. Look out too for decorative *yarmulkes* (skull caps) and some creative uses of the Star of David.

Oriental wares: In the *souqs* you will find all the favourite wares of the Middle East, such as leather goods, brass and copper, *nargilas* (hubble-bubble pipes), and of course carpets and kilims.

The mountains of Jordan make a dramatic backdrop for dinghy sailing off Eilat.

Wood carvings: At any religious site you will find wooden religious statuettes being sold, either in shops or by itinerant vendors.

SPORTS

Israel may not appear to be an obvious place to go for a sporting holiday, but this young and energetic country has dramatic open spaces, miles of accessible coastline, and a burgeoning range of sporting facilities and events, from white-water rafting in the Golan to world-class scuba diving in the Red Sea. The Israelis' own sporting passions are basketball and football (soccer). Look in the local press (see page 119) for details of upcoming matches.

Land-based Activities

Golf: It surprises many visitors that there is only one 18-hole course in Israel, in Caesarea (tel. 06-361174).

Horseback riding: The grassy valleys and gentle slopes of the Sea of Galilee provide classic horse-riding terrain.

Riding centres are to be found near Tiberias at Vared Hagalil, Kfar Hitin (tel. 6-693 5785).

On the coast you can try the riding centre at Caesarea (Herod's Stables; tel. 06-636 1260), while the Artists Village Riding Centre (tel. 04-984 1828) at picturesque Ein Hod, near Haifa, offers the spectacular scenery of the Carmel National Park, Haifa, and the coast.

From Eilat, you can reach the Negev by horse in a few minutes (Texas Ranch; tel. 07-637 6663). Finally, there are even stables in Jerusalem (tel. 02-538 0296).

Hiking: Israelis are great hikers, and almost everywhere you go you will find excellent walking-tour guides. The Society for the Protection of Nature in Israel (SPNI) offers environmental hiking tours nationwide in dramatic settings such as the Samaria Desert, Wadi Qelt, the Dead Sea, Galilee and the Golan, and around Eilat. Call (03) 638 8677 for details.

Similar tours are led by Nature's Way, an organization based in Eilat. You can get their leaflet from the tourist office or by calling (07) 637 0648. They also provide expert advice on independent hiking in the Eilat Mountains Reserve and in the Sinai.

Snow Skiing

Conventional skiing may be the last activity you would expect to find in Israel, but between December and mid-April Mount Hermon offers snow some 2 to 3 metres (6–10 feet) deep on its highest slopes. Chair lifts convey you to the summit (2,021 metres/6,630 feet) and the ski runs. In the summer, hill walkers can enjoy magnificent panoramic views from the mountain.

Snuba is a great way to see what's in the Red Sea.

Hikers should also consider the strange moon-like surface of the Makhtesh Ramon crater (see page 73). Ask at the Visitor Centre for details.

Watersports

Windsurfing: The equipment you need for windsurfing can be hired from the beaches at Tel Aviv (marina), Netanya, Haifa (at Bat Galim beach), Tiberias, and Eilat.

Waterskiing: This is slightly less popular, but there are facilities in Tel Aviv, which has a mechanical pull (Southern Park; tel. 03-739 1168), and Eilat, which offers the full range of motorized watersports, including jet skis, parasailing, and water bananas. All the Eilat activities can be booked through Red Sea Sports (see Scuba Diving, below).

Sailing: Dinghies are available for hire from the marinas at Tel Aviv, Jaffa, Akko, Netanya, and Nahariya.

On the other side of the country, sports are available on the Sea of Galilee and the River Jordan. In the Golan region try white-water rafting through Kibbutz Kfar Hanassi, near Rosh Pinna (tel. 06-06-691 4992), or at Activity Rafting & Recreation (tel. 06-693 9377); try a kayak or go inner-tubing on the Jordan River at Park Hayarden (Abukayak; tel. 06-06-922 245) or at Kibbutz Kfar Blum, tel. 06-694 8755.

Scuba diving: Diving in the Red Sea at Eilat is without doubt the sporting highlight of Israel. This is one of the richest areas in the world for tropical fish and corals, and has excellent underwater visibility, ranging from 15 to 40 metres (50 to 130 feet) and more. There are many diving schools, all of which dive from Coral Beach. The most experienced is Aqua Sport (tel. 06-633 4404). Red Sea Sports are also recommended (tel. 06-637 6569 or 633 3666).

If you want to know what to expect before you dive, visit the Coral World underwater observatory to see the brilliant, teeming underwater life that awaits you in the nature reserve. You can of course enjoy yourself by snorkelling on the surface, or you could try Eilat's unique snorkelling/scuba hybrid "snuba" (see box below). Another Eilat highlight is the opportunity to dive with the dolphins at Dolphin Reef.

An experienced diver may prefer moving onto the Sinai, where the diving is even better.

There are several diving schools along the Mediterranean coast (at Tel Aviv, Haifa, Akko, Rosh Hanikra, and other sites —see tourist offices for details). Conditions are good, with average visibility on calm days of 10 metres (33 feet).

Swimming: You must be careful if swimming along the Mediterranean coast, as many lives are lost here each year to the vicious undertows. You should be safe as long as you obey the beach flags. A white flag tells you it's safe and that a lifeguard is present. A red flag means that swimming is

Snuba

If you enjoy snorkelling and would like to dive deeper without spending time and money learning to scuba dive and without having heavy diving tanks strapped onto your back, then check out Eilat's latest invention, snuba diving. This hybrid, which uses air lines attached to diving tanks floating on the surface, with a marker flag, allows you to dive down to 6 metres (20 feet) with a qualified supervisor. It's open to anyone aged 10 and over, and is offered by two companies, Snuba, on Coral Beach, and Nargila, at Dolphin Reef.

dangerous and a black flag means that no swimming is allowed. At Tel Aviv, there is a pleasant, though expensive, lido by the marina.

Other Activities

Archaeological digs: If you want to lend a hand to those delving into the past, contact either the Youth Section Promotion Department at the Ministry of Tourism (tel. 02-623 7311) or the Israel Antiquities Authority (tel. 02-560 2627). Be warned that the work is often hard, the conditions spartan, and the financial reward nonexistent; but the satisfaction can be immense. You can also arrange archaeology-related expeditions through the Israel Archaeological Society, based in Los Angeles (toll-free in the U.S.A.: 800-ISRAEL-8).

Birdwatching: Eilat enjoys a prime location on the migration path for birds flying from Europe and Asia to Africa. It is therefore one of the best spots in the Middle East from where ornithologists can watch the massive flypast of several hundred bird species. Migration takes place from September through November and from March through May. Contact the International Birdwatching Centre (tel. 07-637 4276) for further information and details of tours and lectures.

Camel treks: Several trekking companies offer the opportunity to explore the Negev Bedouin-style, aboard a camel. The Camel Riders company north of Eilat (tel. 07-637 3218) offers tours that range from 2 to 15 days. If this is too long, there are shorter tours. The Texas Ranch in Eilat (tel. 07-637 6663), for example, organises half-day desert tours daily. Other camel contacts are Desert Breeze (tel. 07-633 7222), Jeep See (tel. 07-633 0130), and Tracks (tel. 03-691 6103).

Desert safaris: Avi Desert Safari in Eilat (tel. 07-637 8024), has been leading off-road jeep safaris into the Sinai, Negev, and Judean deserts for over 20 years.

If you would like a more novel, self-drive way of exploring the desert, hire a Quad Runner. A cross between a motorbike and a small tractor, these fun vehicles are available from the Ostrich Farm at Eilat (tel. 07-637 2405). You must be 18 or over and have a clean driving licence.

ENTERTAINMENT

Jerusalem Nightlife

Jerusalem has a staid reputation, but take a stroll in the New City in the area around Ben Yehuda Street and Yoel Salomon Street and you'll find lots going on most evenings, including

Calendar of Events

For a full listing of all festivals, ask your nearest Israeli tourist office (see page 123) for a copy of *Israel Events*. Remember also to ask them for confirmation of the exact dates.

March–May	*Sea of Galilee:* Festival, with a variety of musical events.
May–June	*Jerusalem:* Israel Festival, with music, dance, theatre, mime, and circus.
June/July	*Jerusalem:* International Film Festival, taking place at the Cinematheque.
July	*Nationwide:* International Folklore Festival. *Haifa port:* Popular blues Festival. *Karmiel:* Israel Folklore Dance Festival.
August	*Eilat:* International Red Sea Jazz Festival.
November	*Nationwide:* International Guitar Festival.

a handful of discos, several music bars and "pubs," and narrow streets congested with tables and thronging with locals and tourists.

Three venues regularly put on Israeli **folklore** shows. The YMCA Auditorium, on King David Street (tel. 02-624 7281), produces an entertaining song-and-dance show on Monday, Tuesday, and Saturday evenings; the Khan Theatre, in Remez Square, near the railway station (tel. 02-671 8281), stages regular folklore shows in an old *caravanserai,* as well as hosting a theatre and the city's one and only nightclub; the Kiryat Anavim Kibbutz Hotel (11km/7 miles out of town; tel. 02-534 8999) hosts an enjoyable evening of dance every Friday with music of the 1960s. Other minor venues stage occasional ethnic folk-music concerts.

In the summer, the Sultan's Pool, a vast outdoor amphitheatre, stages rock concerts or other big-name events.

Jerusalem **theatre** is varied and eclectic, but most productions are in Hebrew. The Jerusalem Centre for the Performing Arts (Jerusalem Theatre) at 20 Marcus Street hosts local and foreign productions of theatre, opera, and dance. The Centre also houses a bookstore, coffeehouse, restaurant, and cinema. The box office (tel. 02-561 0011) is open Sunday through Thursday from 10:30 A.M. to 1:00 P.M. and one hour before performances.

Among the venues for **classical music** are churches, museums, the Givat Ram University campus, the Jerusalem Theatre, and the Henry Crown Auditorium.

There are several **cinemas,** showing films in their original language with subtitles in Hebrew. The Cinematheque, Hebron Avenue (tel. 02-672 4131), is the best venue for film buffs.

For information about nightlife, look in *Time Out*, the listings pull-out section of the *Jerusalem Post*, which is published every Friday. Also excellent is *Your Jerusalem*, a free monthly newspaper which you can pick up in hotels and various tourist haunts. (See Media on page 119)

Tel Aviv Nightlife

In contrast to Jerusalem, Tel Aviv comes alive at night. Crowds congregate along the promenade and along Dizengoff Street, but there's much more to do than just people-watch. If you're after bars and **nightclubs,** look in *This Week in Tel Aviv* (a free listings magazine). There are over 20 nightclubs to choose from, some of them offering Greek, Oriental, or Jamaican themes. In neighbouring Jaffa there are more nightspots offering touristy Oriental folklore entertainment.

If you are keen to learn Israeli **folk dancing,** the Bicurei Ha'etim Cellar in Heftman Street (tel. 03-691 9510) will teach you.

There is a good choice of **cinemas,** showing mainstream English-language films.

Those with more highbrow tastes should make for the Tel Aviv Performing Arts Centre, Leonardo Da Vinci Street (tel. 03-692 7777). **Opera** lovers can enjoy the acclaimed New Israel Opera company here or at the Cameri Theatre, Dizengoff Street (tel. 03-523 3335/527 9888). The Cameri is also the only **theatre** in town to regularly stage productions with a simultaneous English translation (every Tuesday night). The Habima Theatre, Habi-

Stepping out, Israeli folk-style, at the famous YMCA Auditorium, Jerusalem.

ma Square (tel. 03-526 6666), is claimed to be the country's best repertory theatre. It occasionally puts on English-language performances.

Lovers of **classical music** should make for the Mann Auditorium, Hubermann Street (tel. 03-528 9163), or the Tel Aviv Museum of Art, Shaul Hamelech Boulevard (tel. 03-696 1297). The Israel Ballet Company is based in Tel Aviv. **Dance** is also staged at ZOA House, Daniel Frisch Street (tel. 03-695 9341).

To find what's on in general consult the *Time Out* supplement of the *Jerusalem Post* on Fridays, *This Week in Tel Aviv,* and *Tel Aviv Today,* a particularly good free monthly magazine. (See MEDIA on page 119.)

Eilat Nightlife

The Mediterranean-style resort nightlife of this popular spot appeals most to the young and "young-at-heart," namely those who thrive on lively (and loud) international pubs, bars, and discos. If you want more serious entertainment, this is not the place for you.

Much of the action is hotel-based, though the new commercial centres in the town are also very busy. There is nothing recognizably local in the tourist areas, except for the rather bland Israeli **folklore** shows staged in the hotels. If you prefer a livelier and more authentic experience, try the popular Bedouin Evening at the Ostrich Farm, which includes belly dancing and story-telling (tel. 07-637 2405).

Fringe films in English are screened at the Cinematheque at the Philip Murray Centre, Ha'Temarim Boulevard, and there is a Creative Arts Centre (opposite the port) where occasional musical events are staged. The highlight of Eilat's musical year is the International Red Sea Jazz Festival (see page 89).

For more information, pick up the monthly listings leaflet, *Events and Places in Eilat,* from the tourist office. (See MEDIA on page 119.)

CHILDREN'S ISRAEL

Jews and Arabs share a love of children and welcome them almost everywhere. Nevertheless, the Holy Land is not the ideal place for a family holiday. Not many children will enjoy visiting more than the occasional holy or historical site, especially if they have to keep silent. Careful planning and an imaginative approach to relating the story behind a site could, however, make a huge difference in stimulating a child's interest.

Israeli **museums** are usually modern, lively places. The Diaspora Museum and Museum of Art in Tel Aviv and the Israel Museum in Jerusalem all have youth sections with exhibits and activities.

The **resorts** on Israel's west coast don't particularly cater for children, though Eilat is a typically Mediterranean-style resort with numerous beach activities and hotels designed with European families very much in mind.

At **night,** folklore shows are a good bet for older pre-teens and perhaps young teenagers (see opposite page). For some-

Meeting the dolphins at Dolphin Reef in Eilat is both fun and educational.

thing more "high-tech," Eilat offers *20,000 Leagues Under the Sea* aboard the *Jules Verne* mobile underwater observatory boat. This is a spectacular laser-assisted special-effects underwater adventure. For entertainment on a more intimate scale, Eilat stages a Bedouin Evening (see page 92).

Eilat is the place for **water activities.** Older children can learn to windsurf or try Eilat's own snuba diving (see page 87). Coral World's Yellow Submarine may well be the highlight of a child's holiday, but make sure you know the cost before you suggest it. Pedalos are a good starting point.

Wildlife: There are no major zoos in Israel. Even so, the Biblical Zoo in Jerusalem, the Dolphinarium in Tel Aviv, the Llama and Alpaca Farm at Mitzpe Ramon, the alligator farm at Hammat Gader near the Sea of Galilee, and the Hai Bar Biblical Nature Reserve near Eilat should all prove popular.

In Eilat itself dolphins are the big attraction for visitors. Dolphin Reef (see page 76) is an excellent family attraction, and children can actually swim or even dive with the dolphins (at a cost). Children of all ages will also love the fabulous colours and shapes of the creatures of the deep on display at Coral World (see page 76) or viewed from aboard one of Eilat's special floating observatory boats. To get the best from Coral World, pick up a copy of their excellent full-colour *Fish Guide* and see how many of the 745 different fish and corals your children can identify through the observatory windows.

Finding out what's on: A children's section appears in the *Time Out* section in each Friday's *Jerusalem Post* and in *Your Jerusalem* (see MEDIA on page 119). There are story-telling sessions for children (from three years upwards), a puppet theatre, and other events for English-speaking children in Jerusalem. However, many activities are in Hebrew only.

EATING OUT

There is no such thing as "Israeli cuisine," but in magpie style the country has gathered an enormous selection of types of foods and restaurants from around the world, most obviously from those countries in which Jews have settled. Oriental cuisine, which means a Middle Eastern style of cooking embellished with many Arabic influences, is also widely available.

WHERE TO EAT

Because of kosher regulations there are two main types of restaurant—meat and dairy. A meat restaurant has various animal cuts on the menu, but is not allowed to serve any milk-based products with them (e.g., steaks or chops cooked in cream sauces are forbidden). These regulations are by-passed by the use of non-dairy sauces and non-dairy cream-ers for tea and coffee; even non-dairy ice creams have been developed to avoid the problem.

Many dairy restaurants are informal and styled like cafés. They are largely vegetarian, serving soup, pasta, vegetable pies, quiches, and of course salads, which are of invariably good quality and come in generous portions. Most dairy restaurants also serve a limited fish menu, usually featuring salmon, trout, and sole.

For a selection of recommended restaurants in Israel, see our list, starting on page 137. If you are staying in Tel Aviv or Jerusalem, get a free copy of *Tel Aviv Menus* or *Jerusalem Menus*, two very useful booklets which feature short descriptions and menus of the city's most interesting restaurants (your hotel should have copies). Many restaurants featured in these publications also offer a discount on production of the booklet.

WHEN TO EAT

The majority of dairy restaurants stay open throughout the day and late into the night or early next morning, particularly on Saturday. Many of the more formal meat restaurants are also open all day, though traditional hours are approximately noon to 3:00 P.M. and 6:00 or 7:00 P.M. to 11:00 P.M. Numerous (but by no means all) restaurants stay closed for the Sabbath from Friday afternoon until Saturday evening.

Fresh ingredients for preparation—there are few secrets in this Jerusalem restaurant kitchen.

WHAT TO EAT

Oriental Cuisine

In any Arab town or quarter in Israel you will find restaurants, stalls, and street vendors selling *shishlik* (shish kebabs), offal, *shwarma* (doner-kebab, which is pressed lamb sliced off a vertical revolving spit), and the ubiquitous *hummous*. This renowned Middle Eastern staple food is created from chickpeas puréed with sesame-seed oil. It is invariably served with pitta bread, and you can often get it topped with *foul* (which are a kind of beans, the word itself being pronounced "fool"), pine kernels, and/or meat. The best *hummous* is said to be served in the Muslim Quarter of Old Jerusalem, where you will find basic cafés specializing in *hummous* with only one or two other dishes. Meat may be served in pitta pockets on its own, leaving you to fill the rest of the pitta yourself from a colourful selection of salads, pickles, and spicy sauces to suit your own taste.

Diaspora Cuisine

In the restaurants of Jerusalem and Tel Aviv you will find French, Italian, Spanish, Hungarian, Romanian, Moroccan, Lebanese, Ethiopian, Indian, South American, and Chinese among the various national cuisines that are represented. Some of these reflect the influence of the Diaspora, others simply reflect the demands of tourism and big city international food trends and fads.

Jewish cooking, as it is perceived in Europe, is usually of Eastern European (Ashkenazi) origin. This is a heavy cuisine typified by soups (particularly chicken), schnitzels, *blintzes* (pancakes), *gefilte fisch* (fish and matzo meal balls poached), and stews. If you eat in a Jewish restaurant on the Sabbath (most are closed) you may be offered *cholent* (pronounced "chunt"), a particularly heavy meat-and-bean stew.

A favourite Diaspora-type food is Yemenite cuisine, such as a *mallawach*, which is a fluffy pancake filled out with chunks of spicy meat or chicken and served with sauces.

Kosher Food

Kosher simply means that food has been prepared in accordance with Jewish dietary laws. Its best known injunction is that meat and dairy products must not be served together. The Bible declares that a kid must not be seethed (i.e., boiled) in its own mother's milk. Jews do not eat pork, as they regard it unclean, and because seafood must have scales and fins to be kosher, shellfish are also out of bounds.

Pulses, nuts, and fruits are among the cornucopia to be found in any Israeli street market.

Fish

Fish restaurants tend to be expensive and kosher ones don't serve shellfish. Indigenous fish to look for are Buri from the Red Sea, Denis from the Mediterranean, and St. Peter's fish from the Sea of Galilee (see page 58). Most dairy restaurants also serve fish (see above).

Desserts

There isn't really a true Israeli dessert, though do try *khalva*, a sweet, soft, nougat-like confection made of sesame seeds (available from sweet shops). Eastern European *blintzes* (or pancakes), which are served with chocolate, fruit, and/or nuts, might be to your taste. Arab sweets offer more possibilities, all of them dripping with sugar. *Burma*, also known as *baklava* (shredded wheat with pistachios and hazelnuts soaked in honey), is the most familiar dish. Or try the rose-scented *mohalabiyeh* or *malabi,* a blancmange-like dessert, rather like drinking perfume.

DRINKS

Israeli wines, which are mainly produced in the Golan and Haifa (Carmel) areas, are invariably good, as are Israeli lager-style beers, such as Gold Star and Maccabee. Finish off your meal with a *sabra*, Israel's own delicious chocolate-orange liqueur. Remember that devout Muslims do not drink alcohol, so if you are in an Arab establishment, try to see what is on offer before you make a *faux pas*.

Malt Star sounds like, looks like, and even tastes quite like a dark, sweet beer, but it's completely non-alcoholic and a favourite adult soft drink. Fruit juices, sometimes referred to as nectars, are usually quite expensive. You will find internationally popular soft drinks and bottled waters anywhere.

Always say whether you want milk or lemon with your tea, otherwise it will be served black. Ordering coffee can be a fraught business. You won't be offered the Arabic-Turkish variety in Israeli places, and what constitutes "cappuccino" and "with milk" varies wildly. An "Israeli cappuccino" is usually topped with a mountain of whipped cream. Most good places do serve filter coffee, however. Arab coffee is generally dark, strong, and thick. Don't drain the cup unless you want a mouthful of grounds. In tourist places you may get milk. Some Arab and Yemenite places flavour their coffee with cardamom, which is worth a try. Arab tea is always served black.

Falafel

If there is an Israeli national dish and one thing in the country that unites Arabs and Jews, it's *falafel*—deep-fried balls of seasoned ground chickpeas, commonly served inside a pitta pocket. It is the seasoning that makes or breaks a good *falafel*, but at best it's quite a bland snack, and half of its interest comes from the salad, sauces, or pickles you add to it. Falafel stalls, prominent on main pedestrian streets in most towns, provide a cheap and wholesome way of filling up.

To Help You Order ...

| Could we have a table? | **Efshár lekabél shulkhán?** |
| I'd like a/an/some ... | **Ten li, bevakashá ...** |

beer	**bíra**	mustard	**khardál**
bread	**léchem**	pepper	**pilpél**
butter	**khemá**	potatoes	**tapukhéy-adamá**
cheese	**gviná**	rice	**órez**
coffee	**kafé**	salt	**mélakh**
fish	**dag**	soup	**marák**
fruit	**peyrót**	sugar	**sukár**
ice-cream	**glidá**	vegetables	**yerakót**
lettuce	**khása**	water	**máyim**
milk	**khaláv**	wine	**yáyiná**

... and Read the Menu

báklava	sweet flaky pastry with nuts
faláfel	spiced, fried chickpea paste
gefilte fisch	chopped stuffed carp
kavéd of	chicken liver
kebáb	roast lamb or mutton, or grilled ground meat
khálva	honey, almond, and sesame cake
khamuzím	pickled vegetables
khúmus	chickpea purée
kréplakh	dough envelopes with a savoury filling
kúsa	marrow (zucchini) squash
lében	yoghurt
mohalabíyeh	milk and rose-water pudding
piláf	Turkish-style rice
pilpél memulá	stuffed peppers
píta	flat bread
shashlík	skewered meat and vegetables
shnítzel	veal or turkey, breaded and fried

INDEX

Acre 9, 15, 23, 53, 56-57
Aerodium 77
Akko 9, 15, 23, 53, 56-58, 82, 86-87
Ashkelon 52
Avdat 74

Baha'i Shrine and Gardens 54
Banias 66
Basilica of the Annunciation 8, 60
Beersheba 72-73
Bene Hezir 37
Bethlehem 8, 13, 41-43, 82
Bible Lands Museum 40

Caesarea 23, 50-52, 84-85
Capernaeum 63
Carmel 10, 47, 53, 55-56, 85, 98
Caro 65
Chamber of the Holocaust 38
Chapel/Mosque of the Ascension 35
Church/Abbey of the Dormition 37
Church of All Nations 36
Church of Dominus Flevit 34
Church of St. Anne 30
Church of St. Gabriel 61
Church of St. Peter 50
Church of St. Veronica 28
Church of the Assumption 35

Church of the Holy Sepulchre 8, 28-29, 32, 43
Church of the Multiplication of the Loaves and Fishes 63
Church of the Nativity 8, 42
Church of the Pater Noster 34
Clandestine Immigration and Naval Museum 53
Coenaculum 37
Convent of the Sisters of Zion 28
Coral Beach 23, 76, 87

Dagon Grain Silo 54
Dalait el-Carmel 56
Damascus Gate 30-31, 33, 38
David Street 22, 25-26, 90
Dizengoff Street 47, 82, 91
Dolphin Reef 76, 87, 93-94
Dome of the Rock 8, 15, 23-25, 34
Druse Villages 56, 82
Ecce Homo Arch 28

Eilat 9, 21, 23, 72, 74-77, 79, 83-89, 92-94
Ein Gedi 69
El Deir 80
El Khazneh 78
El-Aksa Mosque 8, 15, 24
El-Mahmoudia Mosque 49
Elijah's Cave 53
Eretz Israel 48

Ethiopian Convent 28

Franciscan Grotto 35
Franciscan oratory 28

Garden of Gethsemane 23,
    35-36
Garden Tomb 23, 32
Golan Heights 18-19, 66
Grotto of the Manger 43

Ha'Ari 65
Hadar 54-55
Hagana Museum 47
Hai Bar Wildlife Reserve 74
Haifa 10-11, 17, 20, 53-56,
    82, 85-87, 89, 98
Hammat Gader 64, 94
Herod's Family Tomb 39
Herodian 26, 43
Herzliya 52
Hisham's Winter Palace 44
Hof Argaman 58
Hurva Synagogue 26

Isfiya 56
Islamic Museum 25
Israel Museum 39-40, 48, 69,
    82, 92-93

Jaffa 22, 32-33, 38-39, 44-50,
    66, 82-83, 86, 91
Jericho 10-12, 20, 42-44,
    47, 66
Jerusalem Street 31, 65, 82, 90
Jewish Quarter 26

Kedumin Square 50
Khan el-Umdan 58
Kidron Valley 36
Kikkar Zion 38
King David Hotel 39
King David's Tower 16, 22
King Solomon's copper mines
    12, 74
King Solomon's Pillars 74
Knesset 40

Lake Kinneret 62
Liberty Bell 39
Lion Fountain 39
Louis Promenade 55

Mane Katz Museum 56
Manger Square 42
Mary's Tomb 23, 35
Mary's Well 61
Masada 9, 14, 19, 23, 43, 70-71
Megiddo 47, 61
Milk Grotto 43
Mitzpe Ramon 72-73, 94
Monastery of St. Catherine 80
Monastery of the Cross 40
Monastery of the Flagellation
    28
Monastery of the Temptation
    43-44
Mosque of El-Jezzar 23, 56, 58
Mount of Olives 8, 21, 23,
    33, 35
Mount of the Beatitudes 62-63
Mount Zion 37-38

Muhraka Carmelite Monastery 56
Museum of Jaffa Antiquities 50
Museum of the Diaspora 48, 93
Museum of the Underground Prisoners 58

Nahariya and Rosh Hanikra 59
National Maritime Museum 53
Nazareth 8, 14, 59, 82
Netanya 51-52, 83, 86
Nimrod's Castle 67

Peace View Park 55
Petra 20, 23, 74, 77-80
Pool of Bethesda 31
Prehistory Museum and Zoo 56

Qumran 68

Rachel's Tomb 42
Rockefeller Museum 33
Roman aqueduct 52
Roman hippodrome 52
Royal Tombs 80
Ruben & Edith Hecht Museum of Archaeology 56

Safed 63-66, 82
Sea of Galilee 23, 58-60, 62, 64, 66, 84, 86, 89, 94, 98
Shalom Tower 46-47
Shepherds' Fields 43

Shrine of The Book 39, 69
Solomon's Quarries 33
St. George's Cathedral 32
St. Joseph's Church 61
Stations of the Cross 27
Stella Maris Carmelite Church and Monastery 54
Synagogue Quarter 26, 65

Tel Aviv 8, 11, 19-20, 44-48, 50-51, 82-83, 86-88, 91-95, 97
Tel Aviv University Museums 48
Tel Jericho 44, 47
Temple Mount 8, 22-25
Tiberias 14, 60, 62-64, 85-86
Timna National Park 23, 74
Tomb of King David 36-37
Tomb of the Prophets 34, 55
Tomb of Zechariah 34, 36
Tomb/Pillar of Absalom 36

Via Dolorosa 8, 26, 29, 31

Wadi Rum 77
Western Wall (Wailing Wall) 18, 23, 25
White-Russian Orthodox Church of Mary Magdalene 34-35

Yad Vashem 9, 40
Yemenite Quarter 47
Yemin Moshe 39
YMCA Building 39

HANDY TRAVEL TIPS

An A–Z Summary of Practical Information

A Accommodation 105
Airports 106
B Bicycle and Moped
Rental 107
Budgeting for Your
Trip 107
C Camping 108
Car Rental 109
Climate and
Clothing 109
Crime 110
Customs and Entry
Formalities 111
D Driving in Israel 111
E Electric Current 113
Embassies and
Consulates 113
Emergencies 114
Environmental Issues
114
Etiquette 114
G Guides and Tours 115
H Health and Medical
Care 115
Holidays 116

L Language 117
M Media 119
Money Matters 119
O Opening Hours 120
P Photography 121
Police 121
Post Offices 121
R Religion 122
T Telephones 122
Time
Differences 123
Tipping 123
Tourist Information
Offices 123
Transport 124
Travellers with
Disabilities 126
Travelling to
Israel 126
W Water 127
Weights and
Measures 127
Women
Travellers 128
Y Youth Hostels 128

A

ACCOMMODATION (See also Camping, Youth Hostels, and Recommended Hotels)

Hotels in Israel are similar to those in any country geared for modern international tourism, and many large international groups are well represented. The pick of the chains is undoubtedly the Dan group, which offers some of the most luxurious hotels in the country. Older accommodations with real character are thin on the ground, with two notable exceptions, the King David (itself part of the Dan Group) and the atmospheric American Colony Hotel, both in Jerusalem.

All hotels are government-inspected, though the standard star rating system has recently been discontinued. The main dining area of most hotels is kosher (see Eating Out, page 95), though large hotels, particularly in Eilat, feature a number of restaurants of varying styles. A buffet breakfast and all taxes are included in the price of a room, which is generally quoted in U.S. dollars, but some hotels also levy an additional and unexpected 15% service charge. You will escape VAT if you pay in foreign currency or by credit card.

Kibbutz guest houses offer a friendlier alternative. Like American motels, these are often situated in out-of-the-way places, never in town centres or resorts. Some are quite luxurious, many have swimming pools, and it's a good way to get a feel of kibbutz life (see Galilee, page 60) without having to work your passage.

If you'd prefer to be in the thick of things, there are other simple bed-and-breakfast options, vetted by the local tourist office, available through private landlords. Christian houses and hospices are another option for budget travellers to Jerusalem and the Galilee. Originally designed for pilgrims and often attached to religious sites, many of these are fairly spartan. However, you don't have to be a practising Christian or have any particular affiliations to be able to stay in these peaceful houses. Ask the tourist office for a list of bed-and-breakfast accommodation and Christian houses. Information on a variety of accommodations can be obtained on the world wide web at www.israelhotels.org.il.

There are three basic seasons for accommodation prices: peak (Christmas, Easter, and other religious holidays, see HOLIDAYS on page 116); regular (late February to mid-November); and low (the rest of the year). However, these also vary according to geography. The peak period on the Mediterranean coast is July and August, whereas this is classified as low season by some Eilat and Tiberias establishments, because of the punishing heat.

During peak times many hotels are full, so book in advance wherever possible. Some tourist offices operate a booking service.

Do you have any vacancies?	**Yesh lakhem ḥadarim?**
I'd like a single/double room.	**Avakesh ḥeder leyaḥid/ḥeder zugi.**
with a bath/shower/private toilet	**im ambatya/miklaḥat/ sherutim pratiyim**
with a balcony/view/air conditioning	**im mirpesit/nof/mizug avir**
What's the price per day/week for bed and breakfast?	**Ma hameḥir leyom/ leshavua/im aruḥat boker?**

AIRPORTS (nemal ha-teufa)

Ben-Gurion, the main international airport, is in Lod, 20 km (12 miles) southeast of Tel Aviv and 50 km (31 miles) west of Jerusalem. Facilities include a 24-hour tourist office, bank, and post office, closed only on holidays and the Sabbath.

United Tours operates regular shuttle buses to Tel Aviv (20 minutes) and Jerusalem (45 minutes), from 4am to midnight. Egged buses leave regularly for Tel Aviv and for Jerusalem, 6:30am–8pm, as well as for Haifa and several other destinations. The next best option is to take a *sherut*—a shared taxi (see TRANSPORT on page 124). Nesher Taxis operate a fixed rate *sherut* service (tel. 02-623 1231 or 625 3233) (see also TRANSPORT). Only take an ordinary taxi as a last resort and then make sure you know the fare in advance.

Many major Jerusalem hotels offer a shuttle service to and from the airport, so ask about this at the time of your hotel booking. Note too that El Al and British Airways offer an advance check-in service on the night before your flight. Pick up details from the airport or from your hotel.

For 24-hour recorded information on Ben-Gurion flight arrival and departure times, call. (03) 973 1112.

International flights also now go direct to **Ovda,** some 60 km (37 miles) north of Eilat. Buses and taxis run regularly to Eilat.

Where are the luggage trolleys?	**Eyfo haagalot?**
Is there a bus into town?	**Yesh otobus haira?**

B

BICYCLE and MOPED RENTAL

This is not recommended in any of the major cities because of the volume of traffic. However, it is a pleasant way of exploring the Galilee region and (to a lesser degree) Eilat.

Check that rates include tax and insurance, and that such rental will not invalidate your own personal insurance. A crash helmet is advisable even on a pedal cycle. You'll find hire companies in Eilat, Tiberias, and many other tourist towns.

I'd like to hire a bicycle/moped.   **Avakesh liskor ofanayim/**
                       ofanayim im manoa.

BUDGETING FOR YOUR TRIP

To give you a rough idea of what to expect financially, here's a list of prices in U.S. dollars ($).

Accommodation. Double room with bath, regular season (March, April, May, September) in Jerusalem: from $60–75; 3-star B&B $45; 3-star hotel $75–125; 4-star $125–200; 5-star $200–300.

Airport transfer. Sherut: Ben-Gurion airport to Jerusalem $10 per person, Ben-Gurion to Tel Aviv $10 per person.

Israel

Car hire. The following rates are per week, including unlimited mileage, but excluding tax, collision damage waiver (CDW) and theft protection (TP) insurance. Allow an extra $16-18 per day to cover these, plus a $10 flat fee if the car is picked up or dropped off at an airport. Group A $200, Group B $260, Group C $330.

Entertainment. Jerusalem YMCA folklore show $15, Eilat Bedouin Evening/Kibbutz folklore evening (both of which generally include transport and meal) $36.

Excursions. Bethlehem/Mount Zion (half-day) $20; Masada/Dead Sea from Jerusalem $60, from Eilat $75; Timna Park (from Eilat only) $36; Petra overnight $140 (camping) to $200 (4-star hotel); one-day hiking tour $50; half-day camel trip $40.

Meals and drinks. Three-course meal in a moderately-priced dairy restaurant, per person, including service, but excluding drinks, $13–25. Beer $2.50; tea or coffee $1.40–2.20; soft drink $2.50; fruit juice $2–3. Snack (hummous, falafel, sandwich) $3.50.

Sightseeing. Most museums and sites $7–10. Special attractions: Coral World, Eilat, 34 NIS; Dolphin Reef, Eilat, 22 NIS; Ein Gedi Spa, Dead Sea, 36 NIS; Masada (including the return trip by cable car) 33 NIS, Petra 20 JD.

Watersports. Windsurfing, board rental per hour $18; jet ski per 15 minutes $25; parasailing per 10 minutes $35; waterskiing per 10 minutes $30; introductory dive $40; one-day introductory diving course (PADI certified) $275, $45 for 25 minutes; mask and snorkel rental $5 per day.

NB: it is always a good idea to pay your hotel bill and most other tourist services (e.g. excursions, car hire, etc.) by credit card or with foreign currency. If you wish to pay by other means you will be charged an additional 17.5% VAT.

C

CAMPING *(kemping)*

There are many official campsites throughout Israel, offering the usual amenities of electricity, hot showers, shops, and café/restaurants. All camps are guarded at night. During local holidays they are full of Israelis, so book ahead. For more information contact: Israel Camping Association, 112 Moshav, Mishmar Hashiva (tel. 03-960 4350 or 960 4524; fax 03-960 4712).

"Wild camping" is possible; however, you should notify the local police or land-owner in advance to head off potential problems.

CAR RENTAL *(skhirat mekhonit)* (See also DRIVING)

Car hire is the best way of seeing the Israeli countryside, although it is very expensive by European standards (coach tours are also quite expensive). There are numerous local and international operators at the airport and in large towns. The largest and often cheapest local operator is Eldan. Luxury cars include cellular phones. They also rent portable phones at reasonable rates. Unlike many operators, Eldan allows you to take your vehicle into the West Bank. Tel: from **U.K.** (0181) 951-5727; from **U.S.A.** (1-800) 938 5000, or within New York state (212) 629 6090.

You must be at least 21 and have held a driving licence for one year, though some companies require drivers to be 24 or over and to have held a licence for two years. You will have to leave an imprint of your credit card or a large cash sum (about $300) as security. An international driving permit is not necessary in Israel, though you will need it if you want to hire a car across the border in Egypt or Jordan. Beware that you will be charged an additional $10 "airport tax" if you return your hire car to the airport.

I'd like to hire a car.	**Birtzoni liskor mekhonit.**
Do you have any special rates?	**Yesh taarifim meyuhadim?**
What's the charge per day/week?	**Ma hamehir leyom ehad/ leshavua?**

CLIMATE and CLOTHING

The weather in Israel is reasonably predictable and seasonal. In the north, it is hot in summer (May–October) and cool in winter. In the south, it is blisteringly hot in summer and still warm in the winter. Jerusalem, lying in the Judean hills, is usually cold and wet in winter.

Spring and autumn are the ideal times to visit, though this is when hotel rates are at their peak. In Eilat and Tiberias it becomes uncomfortably hot during the height of summer, and prices actually fall.

Clothing. Unless you're heading for Eilat (where almost anything goes), you should wear loose cotton shirts and loose cotton trousers in summer. Avoid offending local cultural and religious sensibilities by wearing too little. It's okay to wear shorts in modern Israeli cities or in the countryside, but change to long trousers or a long skirt to visit a holy site. And at some sites you will be asked to cover your head. Cardboard skull caps are provided; women should always carry a scarf.

In the south, especially in summer, you may need to dress sufficiently to avoid getting sunburned and risking skin cancer. So, sunbathe in short doses only. You also need to take care when visiting archaeological sites. Wear a hat and apply plenty of sunblock. Topless sunbathing in public places is officially forbidden. Bring a pullover or jacket in winter and rainwear for the north.

		J	F	M	A	M	J	J	A	S	O	N	D
Jerusalem	°F	53	57	61	69	77	81	83	85	82	78	66	56
	°C	11	14	16	20	25	27	28	30	28	25	19	14
Tel Aviv	°F	65	66	68	72	77	83	86	86	89	84	76	66
	°C	18	19	20	22	25	28	30	30	31	29	24	19
Eilat	°F	70	73	79	87	95	99	103	103	97	92	83	74
	°C	21	22	26	31	35	37	40	40	36	33	28	23

CRIME (See also POLICE)

In general, Israel is a very safe place for tourists. Pickpockets operate in crowded *souqs,* and Eilat also has something of a reputation among backpackers and budget travellers for petty theft. The vast majority of visitors, however, should experience no such problems.

CUSTOMS and ENTRY FORMALITIES

Citizens of the U.K., U.S.A., Australia, New Zealand, and most EU countries need a valid passport for entry into Israel. A three-month visa will be stamped into it when you enter the country, unless you request otherwise. Note that an Israeli stamp in your passport will bar you from entering certain Arab countries who do not recognize Israel (there is no problem with Jordan or Egypt).

Airport security is time-consuming and sometimes tiresome, but always reassuringly tight.

Customs restrictions on entering Israel are as follows: travellers over 17 years old may import duty free 250 cigarettes **or** 250g tobacco, 2 *l* wine and 1*l* spirits. On returning to their own country visitors may import: **Australia:** 250 cigarettes **or** 250g tobacco, 1*l* alcohol; **Canada:** 200 cigarettes **and** 50 cigars **and** 400g tobacco, 1.1*l* spirits **or** wine **or** 8.5*l* beer; **New Zealand:** 200 cigarettes **or** 50 cigars **or** 250g tobacco, 4.5*l* wine **or** beer **and** 1.1*l* spirits; **South Africa:** 400 cigarettes **and** 50 cigars **and** 250g tobacco, 2*l* wine **and** 1*l* spirits; **U.S.A.:** 200 cigarettes **and** 100 cigars **or** a "reasonable amount" of tobacco.

Currency restrictions. You can bring in any quantity of *shekels* and foreign currency. If you intend re-converting large amounts when you leave the country, check with Customs. There are complex regulations on exporting money, but they usually only apply to large amounts and will not affect most visitors.

I'm here on holiday/business. **Ani kan beḥufsha/leasakim.**
I have nothing to declare. **Eyn li dvarim lehatzhir.**

D

DRIVING IN ISRAEL (See also CAR RENTAL)

Driving conditions. Drive on the right and pass on the left. Speed limits are 50 km/h (30 mph) in built-up areas, 90 km/h (60 mph) elsewhere, and 100–120 km/h (60–70 mph) on highways.

Israel

Driving is generally fast and aggressive. In any of the three big cities driving can be a nightmare, and most towns of any size are congested, with confusing one-way systems. Conditions don't improve much until you are well out into the countryside. Motorways link Tel Aviv and Jerusalem and much of the west coast; otherwise, fast highways and dual-carriageways criss-cross the country. If you are heading south, the east coast road is the quickest option. Seat-belts are compulsory for the driver and all passengers.

Parking *(hanaya)*. On-street parking in Jerusalem and Tel Aviv is almost impossible. Your hotel may not accommodate your car, or they may levy a hefty garage charge without advance warning, so check before arrival. Parking illegally will lead to a fine or clamping.

Petrol. Petrol *(benzin)* and diesel *(soler)* are easily obtained at any time, though many service stations close on the Sabbath.

Fluid measures

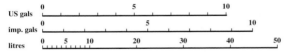

Distance

Road signs. All major road signs are in Hebrew, Arabic, and English, and carry the standard international pictographs. Signs in Hebrew or Arabic only are for local purposes.

Breakdowns. If your rental car breaks down, you must follow the procedures set out in your rental agreement, so make sure you have a copy of this before you set off.

Driving in the West Bank. The official advice is "don't," particularly in Israeli hire cars, as the distinctive Israeli number plates may incite violence. You can go some way towards protecting your parked car by leaving an Arab prayer mat, a copy of the Koran, or an Arab head-dress on the dashboard.

Where's the nearest filling station?	**Eyfo taḥanat hadelek hakrova beyoter?**
super/regular/unleaded	**super/ragil/netul oferet**
My car has broken down.	**Hamkhonit sheli hitkalkela.**

E

ELECTRIC CURRENT

220v/50Hz AC is standard, as in Continental Europe. Sockets usually take three-pronged European plugs. Bring an adapter with you, as they are quite expensive to buy in Israel.

EMBASSIES and CONSULATES *(shagrirut)*

Most embassies are in Tel Aviv; most consulates are in Jerusalem.

U.K.: *Embassy:* 192 Ha-Yarkon Street, Tel Aviv; tel. (03) 524 9171.
Consulates: 1 Ben Yehuda, Tel Aviv; tel. (03) 510 0166 and 19 Nashabibi St., East Jerusalem; tel. (02) 582 8281.

U.S.A.: *Embassy:* 71 Ha-Yarkon Street, Tel Aviv; tel. (03) 519 7575.
Consulates: Nablus Road/Pikud Ha-Merkaz Street, East Jerusalem; tel. (02) 628 2452/628 2231; and 18 Agron Street, West Jerusalem; tel. (02) 253 888.

Australia: *Embassy:* 37 Shaul Hamelech Boulevard, Tel Aviv; tel. (03) 695 0451.

Canada: *Embassy:* 220 Ha-Yarkon Street, Tel Aviv, tel. (03) 527 2929.
Consulate: for visa/immigration, 7 Ha Rav Kook Street, Tel Aviv; tel. (03) 544 2878.

South Africa: *Embassy:* Dizengoff 50 (Dizengoff Tower); tel. (03) 525 2566.

EMERGENCIES (See also POLICE and HEALTH AND MEDICAL CARE)

Police	**100**
Ambulance	**101** (Hebrew)
Fire	**102**

ENVIRONMENTAL ISSUES

You may be tempted to buy exotic souvenirs for yourself and your family on your holiday, but spare a thought for endangered plants and animals which may be threatened by your purchase. Over 800 species of animals and plants are currently banned from international trade and a further 23,000 are controlled by CITES (Convention on International Trade in Endangered Species and Plants). These include many corals, shells, cacti, orchids, and hardwoods as well as the more obvious cats and turtles. So think twice before you buy — it may be illegal, and your souvenirs could be confiscated by Customs on your return.

For further information contact:

U.K.: *Department of the Environmen*t; tel. 01179 878000.
U.S.: *Fish and Wildlife Service*; tel. 001-703 358 2095; fax 001-703 358 2281.

ETIQUETTE (See also TIPPING)

Most Israelis you meet are accustomed to welcoming tourists and, by the very nature of their country, many have a cosmopolitan view of life. The great majority also speak English. Don't be put off by the occasional tout or hustler and don't feel intimidated as a Westerner. Away from the hotter spots of the West Bank, most Arabs are genuinely friendly to Western tourists. In Jewish areas, the greeting is *shalom* (peace); in Arabic areas, it is *salaam.*

Never forget that this is a largely religious country. Respect all holy sites, always cover bare legs and shoulders (see CLIMATE AND CLOTHING), and be wary of photographing people, Jews and Arabs alike, without their permission (see PHOTOGRAPHY). Finally, steer clear of discussing politics or religion.

G

GUIDES and TOURS

You can see most of Israel's major sights with coach tour operators, but this is expensive and not an entirely satisfactory way of getting around. Most tours tend to be the whistle-stop variety and the quality of guides varies. The possession of an official guide badge is no guarantee of competence. If you use an unofficial guide, make sure you agree upon a firm price in advance.

Walking tours, some of them free, operate in Jerusalem (Old City), Haifa, Jaffa, Safed, and Tiberias. Ask for details at your hotel reception desk or at the nearest tourist office.

H

HEALTH and MEDICAL CARE (See also EMERGENCIES)

There is no free health care for visitors to Israel, so make sure you are fully insured before you leave home. Hygiene levels are good, the water is safe to drink, and the standard of medical care is excellent.

By far the most common maladies among tourists, especially in the south, are sunburn and heat exposure. Don't sunbathe for more than 20 minutes at a time, use plenty of high-factor sunblock, drink plenty of liquids, and remember to wear a hat. If you are going on a desert excursion, be particularly careful: take lots of water, emergency food rations, wear the right clothing (including proper shoes), and let someone know where you are. Desert temperatures can plunge sharply at night, so you would be wise to throw a blanket in the boot (trunk) of your car just in case you get stuck.

In summer, take an insect repellent to cope with irritating flies in the desert and with (non-malarial) mosquitoes, particularly in the area around the Sea of Galilee.

For emergency medical and dental treatment call the Magen David Adom (the Red Shield of David), which is roughly equivalent to the Red Cross, call. 101 or 911.

Israel

The *Jerusalem Post* carries listings of those pharmacies and hospitals which are open late or all night.

Vaccinations. There are no compulsory immunization requirements for entry into Israel. However, inoculations against hepatitis A, polio, and typhoid are recommended.

Where's the nearest (all night) chemist?	**Eyfo beyt hamirkaḥat hakarov (hapatuaḥ balayla)?**

HOLIDAYS

There are as many public and religious holidays in Israel as there are religious sects; you could celebrate New Year's Day at least six times a year if you so wished!

The Jewish year is based on a calendar of twelve lunar months (Nissan, Iyyar, Sivan, Tammuz, Av, Elul, Tishri, Heshvan, Kislev, Tevet, Shevat, Adar). Note that this calendar does not correspond to the standard Gregorian calendar used in the West.

On the major holidays and on the first days of Sukkot and Pesach (Passover) all Jewish businesses close.

In Arab areas, many restaurants close for the month of Ramadan.

NB: the following are Jewish public holidays with dates for 1999. For subsequent years these dates should be regarded as approximate.

11–12 September	*Rosh Hashannah* (New Year)
20 September	*Yom Kippur* (Day of Atonement)
25 September– 1 October	*Sukkot* (Feast of Tabernacles/tents commemorating the Exodus)
2 October	*Simhat Torah* ("Rejoicing of the Torah")
4–11 December	*Channukah* (Feast of Lights)

2 March	*Purim*
	(Feast of Esther)
1–8 April	*Pesa(c)h*
	(Passover)
13 April	Holocaust Memorial Day
21 April	Israel Independence Day
21 May	*Shavu'ot*
	(Pentecost harvest festival)

Add to this list Easter and Christmas (the latter is celebrated on 25 December by Christians, on 5 January by Eastern Orthodox churches, and on 19 January by the Armenian church) and various Muslim holidays, in particular the month-long fast of *Ramadan,* during which no Muslim can eat, drink, or smoke between sunrise and sunset; the feast of *Eid-el-Fitr*, which celebrates the end of Ramadan; and the *Prophet's Birthday*. Ask the local tourist office for dates and other details.

Sabbath. The Jewish Sabbath (*Shabat*) starts at sunset on Friday (though businesses close mid-afternoon), lasts until sunset on Saturday, and is still quite strictly observed in Israel. All Jewish businesses, shops, and many (but not all) restaurants close. Nearly all public transport shuts down and few Jews drive their cars on *shabat,* so the city streets are very quiet.

In Orthodox quarters, all work, and even such minor activities as smoking or taking a picture with a camera, are banned. The Muslim holy day is from Thursday sunset to Friday sunset, while Christians observe their day of rest on Sunday.

LANGUAGE

Israel has no fewer than three official languages: Hebrew, Arabic, and English. All tourist information (including restaurant menus) is written in English, and you'll find the language is commonly spoken, as English is taught in schools. Although you won't be expect-

Israel

ed to speak any Hebrew, it is useful and courteous to know a few basic phrases.

Days of the Week

Sunday	**Yom rishon**	Thursday	**Yom hamishi**
Monday	**Yom sheni**	Friday	**Yom shishi**
Tuesday	**Yom shlishi**	Saturday	**Shabat**
Wednesday	**Yom revii**		

Months of the Year

January	**Yanuar**	July	**Yuli**
February	**Februar**	August	**Ogust**
March	**Mertz**	September	**September**
April	**April**	October	**Oktober**
May	**May**	November	**November**
June	**Yuni**	December	**Detzember**

Numbers

0	**efes**	13	**shlosha-asar**
1	**eḥad**	14	**arbaa-asar**
2	**shnayim**	15	**ḥamisha-asar**
3	**shlosha**	16	**shishar-asar**
4	**arbaa**	17	**shiva-asar**
5	**ḥamisha**	18	**shmona-asar**
6	**shisha**	19	**tisha-asar**
7	**shiva**	20	**esrim**
8	**shmona**	30	**shloshim**
9	**tisha**	40	**arbaim**
10	**asara**	50	**ḥamishim**
11	**aḥad-asar**	100	**mea**
12	**shneym-asar**	1000	**elef**

M

MEDIA

Newspapers and magazines. Israelis are voracious readers, and there are plenty of news-stands well stocked with foreign papers and magazines, which usually arrive a few days after publication. The *Jerusalem Post* is the national English-language newspaper, published daily except on Saturday. It's indispensable for keeping abreast of political developments, and it's also a good read. The Friday edition features a useful listings supplement.

There are also many free magazines and newspapers for tourists, including *Your Jerusalem, This Week* (available in Jerusalem, Tel Aviv, and Eilat), *Events* (in Jerusalem, Tel Aviv, and Haifa) and *Hello Israel,* which covers events nationwide. You can get these at tourist offices and hotels, and you could find them at tourist attractions and popular bars. Some have discount coupons.

Radio and Television. There are two Israeli television channels — 1 and 2 — and you may also be able to receive Jordan TV and Middle East TV. All stations feature some programmes and regular news reports in English. Many hotels also have a choice of cable and satellite viewing. The *Jerusalem Post* gives a full listing of all Israeli radio and television programmes and some cable stations. See the Friday edition for a comprehensive guide to local radio programmes and frequencies, including where to find English news and BBC World Service programmes.

MONEY MATTERS (See also CUSTOMS AND ENTRY FORMALITIES)

Currency. The unit of currency is the *New Israeli Shekel* (NIS), usually referred to simply as the *shekel,* divided into 100 *agorot.* Notes come in denominations of 10, 20, 50, and 100 NIS, and coins in 5 and 10 agorot and 1 and 5 NIS.

Israel

Banks and currency exchange. Changing money is expensive at banks, so unless you want to change a reasonable amount (over $150) it is no cheaper than using your hotel cashier.

Licensed money-changers in Jerusalem's Old City give good rates, but never be tempted by black market offers, as you may well be cheated. For banking hours, see OPENING HOURS.

Travellers' cheques and credit cards. Major credit cards are accepted at many retail outlets, petrol stations, and restaurants. U.S. dollar travellers' cheques are most popular (and if you want to take hard currency, many establishments will accept dollars). You will need your passport when you exchange cheques.

I want to change some dollars/pounds.	**Birtzoni lehaḥalif dolarim/ lirot sterling.**
What's the exchange rate?	**Ma hashaar?**
Do you accept credit cards?	**Atem mekabvlim kartisey ashray?**
Can I pay by travellers' cheque?	**Efshar leshalem behamḥaot nosim?**

OPENING HOURS

Banks. Sunday–Thursday 8:30am–1pm and 4–7pm; on Fridays and days preceding Jewish holidays banks generally do not re-open in the afternoon.

Museums. Museums are generally open Sunday–Thursday 9/10am-5pm, Friday 10am–2pm, Saturday closed.

Post offices. Main offices: Sunday–Thursday 8am–6pm (some main branches are open until 10pm); branch offices: Sunday–Thursday 8am–12:30pm and 3:30/4pm–6/6:30pm (some branch offices close Monday and Wednesday afternoon). On Fridays all post offices are open 8am–1/2pm.

Shops. Traditional hours are Sunday-Thursday 8:30am–1pm and 4pm–7pm; Friday and days preceding Jewish holidays 8:30am–1pm. However, many shops now open right through the lunch break.

 P

PHOTOGRAPHY

Major brands of film are more expensive than in the U.K./U.S.A. Photo shops in major towns and Eilat can process your prints in 24 hours or less. Protect your films and camera from the heat and dust.

Check museum regulations before snapping away. Never take pictures in militarily sensitive areas (signs will warn you) and remember that many religious and ethnic groups will not want to be photographed. Always ask permission to photograph someone.

Is it all right to take pictures?   **Mutar letzalem?**

POLICE (See also CRIME and EMERGENCIES)

Israel has a national police force to maintain civil law and order. Uniforms are khaki in summer and dark blue in winter. Most officers speak some English and are quite approachable. Eilat's police have a reputation for being overzealous with jaywalkers.

Jerusalem has a special tourist police force patrolling tourist sites and dealing only with tourist problems. To contact them, dial 100.

Call the police.   **Kra lamishtara.**
I want to report a theft.   **Ani rotze lehodia al gneva.**

POST OFFICES *(doar)*

Post offices handle mail, telegrams, fax, and telephone calls. They are marked by a leaping white deer on a blue background. Most Jerusalem letter boxes are yellow for mail to be sent within the same city, and red for all other mail.

Most main post offices are open Sunday–Thursday, 8am–6pm; branch office hours are usually Monday–Thursday 8am–12:30pm and 3:30/4pm–6/6:30pm. Friday hours are 8am–1/2pm. Some offices also close on Monday and Wednesday afternoons.

Postage stamps are also on sale at many other outlets.

Poste Restante *(doar shamur).* You can have mail addressed to you c/o Poste Restante (general delivery) in whichever town is most convenient. Take your passport along when collecting.

A stamp for this letter/postcard, please.	**Bul bishvil hamikhtav/ hagluya bevakasha.**
Is there any post for me?	**Yesh doar bishvili?**
My name is ...	**Shmi ...**

R

RELIGION

Jews make up over 80% of the population, but Israel is also home to significant populations of Muslims, Samaritans, Christians (Protestants, Catholics, Armenian Orthodox, Eastern Orthodox, Copts), Druse, Baha'is, and various other denominations. All denominations are notionally free to worship in their own ways, maintain their religious and charitable institutions, and administer their internal affairs.

Whatever your religion, you will probably find a place of worship nearby (with the possible exception of Eilat). *Your Jerusalem* and the *Jerusalem Post* list some details of religious services; it's also worth asking at your hotel reception desk for information.

T

TELEPHONES *(telefon)*

For calls within Israel, there are pay phones, which take tokens called *asimonim,* available from post offices, in some shops and hotels, and from street vendors at bus stations.

The country code for Israel is 972. When making calls from outside the country you do not need to dial the "0" that precedes the area code. The "0" preceding the area code must be dialled for calls from other area codes inside Israel.

For **international calls** buy a *telehul* ("call abroad") phone card or go to a Solan telephone kiosk, where you simply make the call on a metered line and pay afterwards.

Useful numbers (see also EMERGENCIES)

Directory enquiries	**144**
Overseas operator	**188**
Telegrams	**171**

TIME DIFFERENCES

Israel is two hours ahead of Greenwich Mean Time in winter, three hours ahead during summer Daylight Saving Time. The following table shows the time difference in various cities.

New York	London	**Israel**	Sydney	Los Angeles
5am	10am	**noon**	9pm	2am

TIPPING

There is no need to leave a tip if the restaurant has levied a 10–15% service charge. Only tip taxi drivers (around 10%) if they have been helpful. Tip room maids and porters according to the service.

TOURIST INFORMATION OFFICES

The Israeli Government Tourist Office (IGTO) has branches in Tel Aviv, Ben-Gurion Airport, and Nazareth. In addition, there are offices run by municipal bodies.

The airport office (open 24 hours daily except Sabbath) will help you find accommodation for the first night only. Other IGTO offices cannot help with accommodation, but many municipal offices will help you find a room.

The principal offices are listed below:

Akko: entrance to Crusader City; tel. (04) 910 251.

Ashkelon: Afridar Centre; tel. (07) 671 0312.

Israel

Ben-Gurion airport: Arrivals Hall; tel. (03) 971 1485.

Eilat: opp. New Tourist Centre, off Arava Road; tel. (07) 637 2111.

Haifa: 18 Herzl Street, Haifa; tel. (04) 666 521.

Jerusalem: 17 Jaffa Road; tel. (02) 628 0382.

Nazareth: 1601 Casa Nova Street; tel. (06) 570 5555.

Safed: 50 Jerusalem Street; tel. (06) 692 0961.

Tel Aviv: 5, Shalom Aleichim Street; tel. (03) 660 259. New Central Bus Terminal, 6th floor, Shop 6108, South Tel Aviv at the terminus of bus routes 4 and 5; tel. (03) 639 5660.

Tiberias: 8 Alhadef Street; tel. (06) 672 5666.

You will also find offices in Jericho and Bethlehem.

IGTO Offices Overseas:

Canada:	180 Bloor Street, ste 700, West Toronto, Ontario M5S 2V6; tel. (416) 964 3784.
U.K.:	180 Oxford Street, London W1N 9DJ; tel. (0171) 299 1111.
U.S.A.:	800 Second Avenue, 16th floor, NY, NY 10117; tel. (212) 499-5600.

On the World Wide Web: www.goisrael.com *or* www.infotour.co.il.

TRANSPORT

Note that all public transport services either stop altogether or are greatly reduced on the Sabbath (see PUBLIC HOLIDAYS).

Air. Israel's internal carrier, Arkia, flies from: Jerusalem to Tel Aviv, Haifa, Eilat, and Rosh Pinna (for the Galilee); Tel Aviv to Rosh Pinna, Eilat, and Masada; Haifa to Tel Aviv and Eilat. Flights are quick with short check-in times, but quite expensive. For schedules, fares, and reservations, call (03) 690 3333.

Buses. Israel has a very extensive bus service. Egged, the national cooperative, is fast, frequent, comfortable, and reliable, with services to just about everywhere, except to certain parts of the West Bank where Arab buses take over. Egged buses are invariably air-conditioned and fitted with sun-blinds. It is possible to reserve seats for long-distance journeys, and this is advisable on Fridays or prior to holidays. Try to avoid rush hours at all times.

For information on schedules, passes, and multi-fare discounts, ask at the information booth in the central bus station: Jerusalem, tel. (02) 304 5555; Tel Aviv, tel. (03) 639 3252 or 638 4070.

Private taxis. All taxis are required by law to have meters and use them. Many drivers "forget" to turn them on, however, or turn them off once you are in the cab, "to give you a special price." Make the driver aware you know the law, and note his cab number so you can report him to the tourist office if necessary.

Many hotels display taxi fares to popular destinations. However, unless you can make sure the driver accepts these fares before you set off, these are not to be relied on.

Taxis may be hailed in the street, called on the phone, or picked up from any of the larger hotels.

***Sheruts*/service taxi.** *Sheruts* are shared taxis, holding up to seven people, plying popular routes both in and between cities, often where there is no bus service. They are 20–25% more expensive than buses, but a lot cheaper than conventional taxis, and it is unlikely that you will be cheated. A set fare is paid to the driver. Just pay the same as everybody else, regardless of your destination.

Trains. Rail travel in Israel is scenic and cheap but of limited use to tourists, as stations are outside town centres. The trains are also outdated, very slow, and cover only a small part of the country (from Jerusalem to Tel Aviv, all of the west coast, and inland via Beersheba to Ein Hatzeva in the northeastern Negev). However, they are cheap, even more so than buses, and they all have a buffet car.

There is one class only and seats may be reserved. For schedules and fares call (03) 693 7515.

Israel

TRAVELLERS WITH DISABILITIES

Wheelchair travellers will find it hard to negotiate most of the country's ancient sites. However, so much of Israel is modern that the general facilities are a reasonable standard for everyone.

For general advice before leaving Britain, contact **RADAR,** 12 City Forum, 250 City Road, London EC1V 8AF; tel. (0171) 250 322, fax (0171) 250 0212.

In the U.S.A., it's worth contacting either **Mobility International U.S.A.,** P.O. Box 10767, Eugene, OR 97440; tel. (503) 343-1284; email at info@miusa.org; and on the WorldWideWeb at www.usa.org; or the **Society for the Advancement of Travel for the Handicapped,** 347 Fifth Avenue, Suite 610, New York, NY 10016; tel. (212) 447-7284, fax (212) 725 8253.

TRAVELLING TO ISRAEL

By Air

From the U.K.: British Airways and Israel's national airline, El Al, offer daily flights from Heathrow to Ben-Gurion; British Airways also fly from Gatwick to Ben-Gurion. El Al flies from Heathrow, Gatwick, and Manchester to Ovda (for Eilat). Flights are expensive, especially compared to northern Mediterranean airfares, so keep an eye open for special offers, particularly from British Airways. Actual flying time from the U.K. is 4–5 hours.

From the U.S.A. and Canada: El Al flies direct to Ben-Gurion from the following cities: New York, Chicago, Boston, Baltimore, Miami, and Los Angeles. Actual flying time is approximately 11 hours from the East Coast and 15 hours from the West Coast.

A number of European airlines also offer New York-Tel Aviv flights including various stopovers.

Charter Flights. Many non-scheduled flights are available from the above airports.

By Sea

Israel's main cruise port is Haifa. The Mano Lines (tel. 04-866 7722), Caspi (tel. 04-876 7444), and Alaluf (tel. 04-867 9633) all offer regular sailings between Cyprus and Haifa.

W

WATER

Tap water is perfectly safe to drink in all but the most inaccessible parts of Israel, though bottled water is available everywhere.

WEIGHTS and MEASURES (For fluid and distance measures, see DRIVING IN ISRAEL)

Israel always uses the metric system.

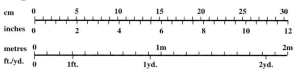

Length

| cm | 0 | 5 | 10 | 15 | 20 | 25 | 30 |
| inches | 0 | 2 | 4 | 6 | 8 | 10 | 12 |

| metres | 0 | | 1m | | 2m |
| ft./yd. | 0 | 1ft. | 1yd. | | 2yd. |

Weight

| grams | 0 | 100 | 200 | 300 | 400 | 500 | 600 | 700 | 800 | 900 | 1kg |
| ounces | 0 | 4 | 8 | 12 | 1lb | 20 | 24 | 28 | 2lb |

Temperature

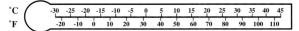

°C -30 -25 -20 -15 -10 -5 0 5 10 15 20 25 30 35 40 45
°F -20 -10 0 10 20 30 40 50 60 70 80 90 100 110

Israel

WOMEN TRAVELLERS

The Middle East is a difficult place for women travellers, so it's vital to be aware of potential problems at all times. In general, Arab and Israeli males suffer from the "Romeo syndrome" that prevails in the Mediterranean. Women should never travel alone in the West Bank and they should always have a male companion if possible. Never hitchhike anywhere in Israel, as this is particularly dangerous, and don't take the "Ramparts Walk" in Jerusalem (see page 33) alone. The best way to avoid problems is to dress conservatively. This doesn't mean being dowdy, but you do need to cover up (short minis or shorts, strapless dresses, and plunging necklines are out).

The good news is that physical assaults are very rare. As long as you take sensible precautions and can cope with the inevitable verbal approaches, there is no reason why you shouldn't enjoy yourself.

YOUTH HOSTELS

There are 31 youth hostels—nine in Jerusalem, two in Tel Aviv, one in Eilat, and the rest scattered around the country. There is no age limit, but many only allow a stay of three nights. They are cheap, clean, pleasant, and offer reasonable meals and accommodation.

An international membership card (obtainable from your own country's association) allows you a small discount.

Ask the national tourist office (see page 123) for a copy of their "Youth Hostels in Israel" map/leaflet, or contact the Youth Hostels Association at the following address: 1 Shazar St., Jerusalem, 91060; tel. (02) 655 8400, fax (02) 655 8431.

Recommended Hotels

Hotels should be booked early for the high season and as far ahead as possible for the regular season (see ACCOMMODATION on page 105).

   The following symbols have been used to denote the price of a double room with bath or shower per night, including breakfast and service, during regular season. These are the highest prices that you are likely to have to pay.

✿	up to 60 NIS
✿✿	60–100 NIS
✿✿✿	100–150 NIS
✿✿✿✿	150 NIS and above

AKKO (ACRE)

Palm Beach Hotel and Country Club ✿✿-✿✿✿ *Akko Beach; Tel. (04) 912 891, fax (04) 910 434.* Acre's finest lodgings, with a beach and the country club's excellent facilities. 110 rooms.

CAESAREA

Dan Caesarea ✿✿✿ *Caesarea; Tel. (06) 626 9111, fax (06) 626 9122.* By the beach, in its own lovely grounds, next to Israel's only 18-hole golf course, this is a sports-lover's paradise. Swimming pool, tennis courts, health club, and many other facilities. 114 rooms.

EILAT

Americana ✿✿ *North Beach; Tel. (07) 633 3777, fax (07) 633 4174.* A popular, well-located hotel with helpful staff, swimming pool, gym, sauna, and jacuzzi. Live entertainment every evening. 137 rooms.

Israel

Dan Eilat ✹✹✹✹ *North Beach; Tel. (03) 362 222, fax (03) 362 333.* Eilat's newest and most luxurious hotel (completed at the end of 1995) with every imaginable facility, including five restaurants, virtual-reality simulators, and lots for children. 382 rooms.

Gazit Menachem (Bed-and-Breakfast) ✹ *Eilat Town; Tel. (07) 633 3326.* Simple, comfortable rooms in the centre of town, a short walk from North Beach. It is run by a friendly and helpful employee of the town's Tourist Information Centre. 3 rooms. You can book at the tourist office.

Riviera Apartment Hotel ✹✹-✹✹✹ *North Beach; Tel. (07) 633 3944, fax (07) 633 3939.* This smart, three-storey complex is ideal for families on a relatively tight budget, and offers a large swimming pool and children's play areas. 172 apartments.

Royal Beach ✹✹✹✹ *North Beach; Tel. (07) 636 8888, fax (07) 636 8811.* Luxurious recent addition to Eilat with large well-equipped rooms, many with wonderful views across the Gulf of Aqaba. Beautiful pool area with waterfalls. Also health club, sauna, Turkish bath, jacuzzi. Ten restaurants, pub, and disco. 375 rooms.

Orchid ✹✹✹✹ *Coral Beach; Tel. (07) 636 0360, fax (07) 637 5323.* Charming low-rise "Thai Village" with cobbled paths, waterfalls, Thai restaurant, and stylish "village-house" accommodation, each with its own verandah. Ask to be set back as far as possible from the main road for the best views and least traffic noise. Fitness room, sauna, Thai massage, free use of bicycles for guests. 132 bungalows.

HAIFA

Dan Carmel ✸✸✸✸ *87 Ha Nassi Avenue; Tel. (04) 830 6306, fax (04) 838 7504.* Tops in every sense in Haifa, with wonderful views over the town and bay. Most of the usual facilities, including a charming garden, swimming pool, and health club. Pub, restaurant. 220 rooms.

Dvir ✸✸ *124 Yefe Nof Street; Tel. (04) 838 9131, fax (04) 838 1068.* The location of this hotel is excellent, affording as it does great views from the front-facing rooms (don't book accommodation in the annex if possible). This is one of the Dan Hotel training schools, so you'll find that the staff try a bit harder. Access to swimming pool. 30 rooms.

JERUSALEM

American Colony Hotel ✸✸✸ *1 Louis Vincent, off Nablus Road, East Jerusalem; Tel. (02) 627 9777, fax (02) 627 9779.* Arguably the most atmospheric hotel in the whole country, occupying a former pasha's palace that dates from 1860. Facilities and attractions include a swimming pool, beautiful gardens, and a tranquil courtyard open for breakfast, lunch, and dinner. Open-air bar, poolside restaurant, dining room. Rooms are decorated in either traditional or modern styles. The superior rooms are well worth the extra charge. 84 rooms.

Beit Shmuel ✸✸ *13 King David Street, West Jerusalem; Tel. (02) 620 3456.* This is a large and modern Orthodox Jewish cultural centre and guest-house complex which enjoys an excellent location with good views of the Old City. There is a friendly atmosphere and staff are helpful. 40 rooms.

Israel

Christ Church Guest House ✿ *Opposite the Citadel, Jaffa Gate, Old City; Tel. (02) 627 7727, fax (02) 627 7730.* Popular haunt with budget travellers. The atmosphere is friendly, and the rooms are basic but clean. Breakfast included in the price of a room. 32 rooms.

King David ✿✿✿✿ *23 King David Street, West Jerusalem; Tel. (02) 620 8888, fax (02) 620 8880.* Israel's best accommodation option, according to many travellers, and usually the first stopping place for visiting heads of state. There is a charming Old-World atmosphere in the reception rooms. Ask for a bedroom facing the Old City walls. The grounds and pools are very beautiful, and the facilities also include a fitness centre. 257 rooms.

Lev Yerushalayim Aparthotel ✿✿✿ *18 King George Street, New City; Tel. (02) 530 0333, fax (02) 623 2432.* The Lev Yerushalayim is a modern block with well-equipped and spacious apartments, situated only a short walk from the heart of the New City. 97 rooms.

Notre Dame Centre, Guest House Section ✿ *Opposite New Gate, Old City, West Jerusalem; Tel. (02) 627 9111, fax (02) 627 1995.* This is a Roman Catholic guest house, but it is open to everyone. The rooms are simple and comfortable, popular with budget travellers. Some rooms have balconies. The building has been beautifully restored, and the food is good. 50 rooms.

Palatin Hotel ✿✿ *4 Agrippas Street, West Jerusalem; Tel. (02) 623 1141, fax (02) 625 9323.* This quiet and small hotel (with both air-conditioning and TV in the rooms) is situated very close to the heart of the New City. One notable feature is the contemporary art featured in public areas and bedrooms. Room price includes breakfast. 28 rooms.

St. Andrew's Hospice ❀ *1 Kikar David Remez; Tel. (02) 673 2401, fax (02) 673 1711.* St. Andrew's Hospice occupies a great location overlooking the Old City, not far from the Khan Theatre and the Cinematheque. The rooms are basic but comfortable; there are lovely gardens, and the staff are friendly. 20 rooms.

YMCA East Aelia Capitolina ❀❀ *29 Nablus Road, East Jerusalem; Tel. (02) 628 6888, fax 627 6301.* The rooms are quite plain and the YMCA East may lack the character of the YMCA West, but it is still very good value in a peaceful setting. Good range of sports facilities, which include a swimming pool and squash courts. Dining room, grill, pub. 55 rooms, 109 beds (14 rooms with balconies).

YMCA West (3 Arches Hotel) ❀❀ *King David Street, West Jerusalem; Tel. (02) 569 2692, fax (02) 623 5192.* Bedrooms and public rooms with plenty of character lie inside this splendid landmark building dating from the 1930s. There is a restaurant and a delightful front terrace. YMCA West also has an indoor swimming pool, four tennis courts, two squash courts, sauna, basketball court, and a fitness room. Price includes breakfast. 56 rooms.

NEAR JERUSALEM

Mizpe Ramat Rachel ❀❀❀ *D. N. Isfon Yehuda 9900; Tel. (02) 670 2555, fax (02) 673 3155.* One of the best kibbutz houses, the Mizpe Ramat Rachel occupies a pleasant site overlooking Bethlehem and the Judean Hills, yet is within a short 10-minute drive of Jerusalem's Old City. Swimming pool, sauna, and fitness room. 250 rooms.

MITZPE RAMON

Ramon Inn ❀❀-❀❀❀ *1 Ein Akev Street; Tel. (07) 658 8822, fax (07) 658 8151.* This new 4-storey hotel uses local furnishings, fabrics, and stone in a successful attempt to create a sympathetic harmony with its stunning natural setting. There is a choice of excellent local ethnic cuisine. Apartments also available. Access to local swimming pool. 96 apartments.

NAHARIYA

Panorama ✹✹ *8 Ha' Ma'apilim Street; Tel. (04) 992 0555.* A low-rise block with fine sea views from its roof-top terrace. Facilities include a pool. Note: half-board may be obligatory during high season.

NETANYA

Maxim Hotel ✹✹ *8 King David Street; Tel. (09) 862 1062, fax (09) 862 0190.* The renovated Maxim Hotel offers good-quality, comfortable facilities, including several reasonably-priced suites, which are handy for families. There are sea views from some rooms and there is also a swimming pool. 90 rooms.

SAFED

Rimon Inn ✹✹✹ *Artists' Quarter; Tel. (06) 920 666, fax (06) 692 0456.* Arguably the best—and perhaps the most historic—hotel in town, with parts dating from the 17th century. There are splendid views, a swimming pool, and extensive grounds. 36 rooms.

TEL AVIV

Armon Ha-Yarkon ✹✹ *268 Ha-Yarkon Street; Tel. (03) 605 5271, fax (03) 605 8485.* This is a small modern hotel, situated opposite the giants, across the road from the beach, and close to the nightspots of Little Tel Aviv. 24 rooms.

Dan Tel Aviv ✹✹✹✹ *99 Ha-Yarkon Street; Tel. (03) 520 2525, fax (03) 524 9755.* It looks dated, but this rainbow-painted beachside monster is still reputed to be the finest hotel in Tel

Aviv. The rooms are particularly comfortable, staff are friendly, and there is a choice of indoor or outdoor swimming pools. Special lounge for sea-view rooms. 285 rooms.

Moriah Plaza Tel Aviv ✵✵✵-✵✵✵✵ *155 Ha-Yarkon Street; Tel. (03) 527 1515, fax (03) 527 1065.* This modern high-rise block is situated on the beach. It may be the recipient of few architectural accolades, but its rooms are comfortable and very well furnished. The staff are friendly and there is a swimming pool. 346 rooms.

Moss Hotel ✵-✵✵ *6 Nes Ziona Street; Tel. and fax (03) 517 1655.* This is a fairly well-equipped hotel in a central location with its own parking (a great asset hereabouts). 70 rooms.

TIBERIAS AND THE GALILEE

Church of Scotland Hospice ✵ *Tiberias; Tel. (06) 672 3769, fax (06) 679 0145.* Comfortable modern facilities are offered in unusual black basalt buildings at the Church of Scotland Hospice, which was constructed a century ago as a missionary hospital. A friendly welcome and a pleasant garden and private beach help to ensure that this place continues to be popular. 46 rooms.

Golan ✵✵ *14 Ahad Ha-Am Street, Tiberias; Tel. (06) 679 1901, fax (06) 672 1905.* This appealing hotel offers excellent value with wonderful views over the Sea of Galilee. Its facilities include a swimming pool and a peaceful garden. Dining room, bar. 98 rooms.

Kibbutz Ein Gev Holiday Village ✵✵ *2 km (1 mile) south of Ein Gev Kibbutz; Tel. (06) 665 8027, fax (06) 675 1590.* These modern cabins come with kitchen, bathroom, and air-conditioning, are set on the Sea of Galilee, and make ideal family holiday homes. There is a good restaurant in the village, in addition to a well-stocked mini-market for self-catering visitors. 100 cabins.

Kfar Hanassi Village ✸✸ *Near Rosh Pinna; Tel. (06) 691 4870, fax (06) 691 4077.* Comfortable rooms with *en suite* bathrooms, kitchenettes, refrigerators, and TV in lodges set amidst wide lawns and comfortable facilities for relaxation or BBQ. Breakfast served in dining room of kibbutz. 28 rooms.

Mizpe Hayamim ✸✸ *Safed-Rosh Pinna Road near Rosh Pinna; Tel. (06) 693 7013, fax (06) 693 7191.* Set in 12 hectares (30 acres) of forest, this charming small country hotel enjoys marvellous views over the Sea of Galilee. Its healthy-living philosophy offers home-made organic foods plus a wholesome diet of massage, yoga, and specialist exercise classes. If that is not enough, there are also swimming pool, jacuzzi, sauna, and gymnasium. 65 rooms.

Nof Ginnosar ✸✸ *9 km (6 miles) north of Tiberias; Tel. (06) 679 2161, fax (06) 679 2170.* The Nof Ginnosar enjoys the reputation of being one of Israel's best kibbutz accommodations, situated right on the Sea of Galilee and set in its own gardens. Facilities offered include tennis courts and a private beach. For watersports enthusiasts there is a good selection of kayaks, windsurfers, and sailing boats for hire. 170 rooms.

Vered Ha-Galil ✸-✸✸ *Korazim-Almagor Junction, 18 km (11 miles) north of Tiberias; Tel. (06) 693 5785.* This ranch-restaurant-guest house is something of a local institution, not to mention a novelty. The Vered Ha-Galil offers the perfect base for a Galilee riding holiday, in charming rustic accommodation. The cooking is good and filling and the hosts are friendly (he's from Chicago).

Recommended Restaurants

Below is a selection of some of Israel's best restaurants, arranged by different price ranges. Book ahead at all times for popular restaurants, and on Saturday night and during holiday periods at all other places. Many restaurants now remain open all week and throughout the day (exceptions are noted in our descriptions of restaurants below).

To give you a general idea of what it is likely to cost for an average three-course meal per person, excluding drinks but including a 10 percent service charge, we have used the following price-range symbols:

❀	below 50 NIS
❀❀	50–80 NIS
❀❀❀	80–100 NIS
❀❀❀❀	over 100 NIS

AKKO (ACRE)

Abu Christo ❀❀–❀❀❀ *Fishermen's Port; Tel. (04) 910 065.* You can choose between the pleasant dining rooms and the waterfront terrace. A reputation for serving the best seafood in town.

EILAT

Country Chicken ❀ *The Tourist Center; Tel. (07) 637 1312.* Don't let the name or rather bland modern appearance put you off; this is good-value, down-to-earth Jewish cooking like Momma used to make (a rarity in Eilat). Fried country chicken, soups, and grills are specialities. Kosher.

Eddie's Hideaway ❀❀–❀❀❀ *68 Almogim Street, off Eilot Street; Tel. (07) 637 1137.* Eilat's best-known restaurant has been serving an inventive menu of meat and seafood dishes

(Shanghai fish, shrimp, and pepper steak specialities) for over 20 years. They serve dinner only. Another treat is the free taxi from your hotel that they provide.

El Gaucho ✿✿✿ *Arava Road; Tel. (07) 633 1549.* Here the beef steaks, veal, and chicken are cooked in the Argentinian style, and then carved and served in generous portions by staff dressed in Gaucho costume. The meat and the chefs are sometimes imported from South America. The background music (occasionally live) and the special decor complete the Latin theme.

Fisherman's House ✿ *Coral Beach; Tel. (07) 637 9830.* Here you can eat all you wish from a buffet of six fish dishes, rice, potatoes, and various salads. If you want somewhere to have a party or to take your family, then this is a good place. Excellent value.

Last Refuge ✿✿-✿✿✿ *Coral Beach; Tel. (07) 637 3627.* This large, smart beachside fish restaurant, serving generous portions of fish and seafood, is located next to a marina. Because of the location and the restaurant's popularity, you must reserve a table. Try to book one on the terrace.

Pago Pago ✿✿✿ *Lagoon, North Beach; Tel. (07) 637 6660.* This popular romantic floating restaurant serves French, Mediterranean, and Far-Eastern food in a relaxed South Seas atmosphere.

Spring Onion ✿ *North Beach, by bridge to Marina; Tel. (07) 637 7434.* This is Eilat's best dairy restaurant, generously serving delicious vegetarian dishes and salads in enormous portions.

Tandoori ✿✿-✿✿✿ *Lagoona Hotel, King's Wharf; Tel. (07) 633 3879.* Popular, award-winning, authentic Indian cooking in pleasant relaxed atmosphere with traditional decor. Meats are specially cooked in *tandoors* (charcoal-fired clay ovens). Indian dancers and musicians. Buffet lunch. Open noon to midnight.

HAIFA

Abu Yusuf's ✹ *1 Ha-Meginim Street, Paris Square; Tel. (04) 866 3723.* Grilled meats, *hummous,* and other Arab staples are on offer at this locally famous, award-winning institution. There's no English sign; just look for a basic eating house with large windows and arches and happy customers.

La Chaumière ✹✹✹ *40a Ben-Gurion Avenue; Tel. (04) 853 8563.* Superb French cuisine, served in an old Arab house.

El Gaucho ✹✹✹ *120 Yefe Nof Street; Tel. (04) 837 0997.* Large portions of Argentine-style meats. See entry under Eilat.

Rondo ✹✹✹-✹✹✹✹ *Dan Carmel Hotel, 85-87 Hanassi Avenue; Tel. (04) 830 6211.* The Israeli and Continental cooking is reasonable, but the real attraction is the fantastic view of Haifa by night. Window seat essential. Dinner only.

HERZLIYA

El Gaucho ✹✹✹ *60 Medinat Hayehudim Street; Tel. (09) 555 037.* Lively South American chain. See entry under Eilat.

Whitehall Steakhouse ✹✹✹ *2001 Mercazim Building, Maskit Street; Tel. (09) 580 402.* Many Israelis swear that these are the best steaks in the country. Help yourself to unlimited salad from the abundant fresh bar.

JERUSALEM

Abu Shukri ✹ *63 El Wad Road, Old City; Tel (02) 627 1538.* Legendary *hummous*, with very little else on the menu. Very basic, with formica-top tables, but clean and accustomed to tourists. Quick service. No alcohol. It is open from 8am to mid-afternoon.

Alumah ✹✹ *8 Ya'Avetz Street, New City; Tel. (02) 625 5014.* Jerusalem's quintessential dairy restaurant, serving excellent vegetarian and fish dishes in a typical, beautifully restored and decorated Jerusalem golden-stone house, with garden patio. Kosher. Closed Sabbath and Saturday evening.

American Colony Hotel ❋❋ *Nablus Road, East Jerusalem; Tel. (02) 627 9778.* Lunch in the leafy, peaceful, sunny courtyard of this famous institution, a former pasha's palace, is a sheer delight at any time, but the Saturday barbeque (summer only) is something special.

Cacao at the Cinematheque ❋-❋❋ *Cinematheque, 1 Hebron Road; Tel. (02) 671 0632.* A vegetarian restaurant serving great pasta, salads, and desserts in a small, modern, arty dining room with views of the Old City walls. Lively, young, buzzing atmosphere. Kosher.

The (Loaves and Fishes) Coffee Shop ❋ *Opposite Citadel, Jaffa Gate, Old City; Tel. (02) 628 6812.* Small pine-panelled café serving excellent cakes, salads, and soups to foot-weary tourists. Young, friendly, Christian staff, quiet relaxing atmosphere to soothe your nerves after a day in the Old City.

El Gaucho ❋❋❋ *22 Rivlin Street; Tel. (02) 624 2227.* Lively South American chain. See entry under Eilat on page 138. This one is housed in a stone building with interior arches and flag-stone floors. Kosher. Closed on Friday.

Kamin ❋❋-❋❋❋ *4 Rabbi Akiva Street, off Hillel Street, New City; Tel. (02) 625 6428.* Delightful, typical old Jerusalem stone house with a charming garden terrace. Mixture of dairy restaurant and international meat dishes, with French flavour.

Kohinoor ❋❋-❋❋❋ *Holiday Inn Crown Plaza; Tel. (02) 581 367.* A member of the Tandoori chain of restaurants, serving excellent Indian tandoori dishes. Kosher.

Mishkenot Sha'ananim ❋❋❋❋ *Yemin Moshe, steps below the Windmill; Tel. (02) 625 1042.* Israel's finest French restau-